almost
The   Effortless Cook Book
^

Pork fillett.

Fry onions, butter add mustard while
Simmer
wine, then cream

About this book

All of us have to eat to live. This book is intended for those who care about the quality and taste of what we eat, but also recognise that life is made up of a number of other essential and desirable activities too!

What is 'effortless' for one cook may seem daunting to another. The compilers hope that this book will encourage those who cook very little but would like to extend their range, as well as offering experienced cooks something of interest.

The Almost Effortless Cook Book includes
- easy recipes,
- other ways of making cooking easier, suggested by our contributors.

The book has been made possible by the willingness of more than seventy people – ranging in age from over ninety to under ten – to share their recipes, and their experience of providing enjoyable meals.

We resist the idea that limiting the effort is somehow cheating. Our attitude is – if the recipe is easy, and the end result tastes good, why not pass it on? That is what this book seeks to do.

Contents

The Almost Effortless Cook Book began life as a slim booklet for a friend who wished to extend his repertoire of easy recipes. This version has been compiled to raise funds for some improvements to St John's Church, Aust, in South Gloucestershire.

Almost effortless cooking?

When you are cooking, effort is of two kinds:

- physical effort: chopping, mixing, stirring and lifting pots and pans;

- the mental effort of deciding how long a dish will take to make, how fast it is cooking, and when it will be ready.

Any skill has to be acquired. If you are wondering whether to give cooking a go, think back on how you reacted when you were learning to decorate, play an instrument, ride a bike, enjoy a sport. Remember your first efforts at DIY or applying make up, learning which products to use, or which manual/beauty editor to rely on (see page 103 for the cookery writers commended by our contributors).

If you are the cook, there is no such thing as an absolutely effortless meal. On pages 104-108 will be found hints to make shopping, storing and clearing up easier. In addition, three of our contributors have generously shared their individual policies on what to keep in store, cooking for one, and eating well on a budget (see pages 109-117).

Cooking terms and processes can sometimes be confusing, for example:

- The famous chef, John Tovey, tells of a complaint about his trademark cheese and herb paté recipe from someone who had mistakenly used a head (bulb) of garlic instead of a single clove.

- When cooking turkeys in foil was first introduced, Fanny Craddock was asked, 'Do I put the butter inside or outside the foil?'

- If you and your flat-mate judge that one shrivelled up bay leaf won't do much for a casserole, and put in half a dozen instead, the result will be inedible. (Take it from one who knows!)

Never think that a question is too foolish, or hesitate to ask for advice from someone whose cooking you enjoy.

Expenditure of effort should not be confused with expenditure of time. **Fast** cooking can require a high degree of mental and physical effort (just watch Professional Master Chef). Conversely, a supper dish put in the oven for 30 minutes or so won't come to any great harm if the 'phone rings and it cooks for an extra few minutes. Many recipes in this book are of this type.

Cooking processes are part of the skill of cooking, which can be as soothing and enjoyable as any craft or skill, provided that judicious use is made of labour saving devices. Experienced cooks know that the quality and suitability of pots, pans and other equipment make all the difference. A list of our contributors' preferred electrical equipment, and their favourite small items can be found on page 101. Over time most people build up the kit which suits them best.

If you are multi-tasking, including cooking the supper, a timer you can sling round your neck or clip on to your clothes is a boon. It is undeniably exasperating to lose track of time so that the food is spoilt.

But keep a sense of proportion: to quote Nigella Lawson, it's not a test of your worth, it's just dinner. Cooking is not a religion. It is not a sin if a dish goes wrong or the cake is a flat failure. It's a pity if the ingredients were expensive, and embarrassing if the gang is expecting something to eat, but virtually all experienced cooks will admit to their off days. When it happens, just substitute something simple, or phone for a fast-delivery pizza, or go out to the pub!

About the recipes. Contributors were asked to supply recipes which they judged easy – tried and trusted favourites, regularly cooked, adopted and adapted. Most contributors live in rural South Gloucestershire, but recipes have come from Scotland to Dorset.

Some recipes are sophisticated; the majority reflect day-by-day cooking for family and friends. Sprinkled among them are suggestions for using up left-overs or making do with what is to hand. Collectively they are a quiet demonstration of the continuing practice of choosing and preparing what you eat, with thoroughly enjoyable results.

Some recipes can be completed in a very few steps, others take longer. It does not follow that the latter are more difficult. No recipe in this book requires specialist culinary skill.

Some recipes are written succinctly – others contain explanatory notes. Small points can sometimes make all the difference.

Almost all recipes in everyday use originated in someone or other's cook book or have been handed down in the family. We readily thank all those cookery writers whose publications have influenced this collection.

Quantities: Judging by our contributors, many cooks still work and think in imperial measurement. In cooking, matching imperial to metric (1oz = 28grams) is not an exact science, as many published cook books confirm. Both 25g and 30g are commonly used as equivalent, sometimes within the same recipe.

Within this book:

- all recipes give metric measurements where such detail is required;

- recipes supplied in both metric and imperial measure are unchanged;

- where recipes were received with only imperial quantities given, metric equivalents have been added (using 25g as the conversion measure).

The majority of recipes quote liquid measure in imperial terms (eg ¼ pint) and these details have been left unchanged.

For most recipes, a few grams one way or the other will not make too much difference. However, with cake recipes it pays to be as accurate as possible.

Oven temperatures: Unless otherwise specified, oven temperatures are for conventional ovens. If you use a fan assisted oven, you will need to decrease the temperature and perhaps the cooking time. (Gordon Ramsay suggests a decrease of 15ºC or 1 gas mark.) The most important thing, however, is to remember that ovens vary, and that sometimes the speed at which a particular recipe is cooked does too. (Read Delia Smith on the timing of baking cakes.) *There is no substitute for making friends with your own oven, getting to know it well.*

Serves how many? Apart from cakes and extras, most recipes are followed by an indication of how many people can be served. Please regard the number given as a suggestion only, not set in stone. With some recipes the ingredients can easily be doubled or trebled.

A note on safety: health and safety anxieties sometimes act as a deterrent to home cooking. This subject is outside the scope of this book; for anyone seeking re-assurance, it is worth knowing that the Food Standards Agency publishes a leaflet on the subject (www.food.gov.uk). Or try your local authority (for example, in South Gloucestershire, the e-mail address is FoodAndHealth@southglos.gov.uk).

Starters

2 dessert pears
4oz (100g) Stilton cheese
1 eggcup of port
4 teaspoons of vinaigrette

Serves 4

Pears with Stilton

- Peel, halve and core the pears.
- Mix Stilton with port and divide into four.
- Spoon Stilton mixture into pear halves, place on a bed of lettuce and chill.
- Just before serving, pour one teaspoon of vinaigrette over each pear half.

Smoked mackerel paté

300g (12oz) smoked
   mackerel
150ml (¼ pt) soured cream
200g (8oz) cottage cheese
2-3 teasp horseradish
   sauce
juice of ½ lemon

- Remove skin and any bones from the mackerel.
- Place all ingredients in a blender and liquidize until smooth.
- Turn into individual small dishes.
- Chill and serve with lemon slices.

Serves 6. Freezes well

Trout paté

8oz (200g) cooked trout
4oz (100g) garlic and herb roulade cheese
2oz (50g) cottage cheese
horseradish cream sauce, to taste
butter

Serves 4 - 6

- Blend trout and cheeses.
- Add horseradish sauce to taste, and blend again to a smooth creamy mixture.
- Put into suitable serving dishes, and cover with melted butter.
- Chill or freeze.
- Serve with toast.

Quick and very tasty warm salad starter

fresh tuna or salmon,
  enough for two
  people
soy sauce, honey and
  lemon juice (or
  ready-made
  teriyaki sauce)
cooking oil
green salad
vinaigrette

Serves 2

- Cut some fresh tuna or salmon into bite size pieces.
- Make a marinade of soy sauce, honey and lemon juice (or could use some ready-made teriyaki sauce) and put the fish in liquid. Leave to marinade for about 30 minutes.
- Heat some oil in a wok and quickly cook the fish for a minute or two until just cooked.
- Place some green salad on individual plates and place the hot fish on the top.
- Add some vinaigrette to the wok to pick up all the flavours left from the fish, heat and pour over the salad.

Philly whizz

Tin of beef consommé*
Packet of Philadelphia
  cream cheese (or
  similar), c.150g

- Place both ingredients in a food processor and thoroughly combine.
- Pour into suitable individual dishes and put in fridge for 2-3 hours.

* The consommé needs to 'set'; look for a tin with gelatine, eg Baxters. *Serves 4*

Soups

Chilled avocado soup

3-4 avocados
1 pt (600ml) chicken stock
½ teasp. salt and pepper
    and sugar mixed.
pinch garlic powder
1 teasp Worcester sauce
½ wine glass of sherry
¼ pint (150ml) double
    cream

- Stone and peel the avocados.
- Put all ingredients, except cream, in a blender and liquidize. Place in fridge for 1 hr.
- Swish in the cream, before serving.

Serves 4

Quick soup – Borscht:

Borscht can be served chilled – the traditional way – or heated through and served hot. Either way the colour is stunning. The word can be spelled several ways.

12oz (325-350g) cooked
  beetroot, peeled
5floz (150ml) soured cream
  or fromage frais
1 pint (600ml) chicken stock
snipped fresh chives to
  garnish

Serves 4-6

- Place the beetroot and half the soured cream (or fromage frais) in a food processor, or blender, and process until smooth.
- Add the chicken stock and process again until smooth.
- Pour into bowl and chill well.
- When completely cold, stir in the remaining soured cream (or fromage frais).
- Serve the soup in individual bowls and garnish with swirl of cream and snipped chives.

Courgette and Boursin soup

3-4 medium courgettes
1 pt (600ml) chicken stock
  (cube is fine)
1 Boursin cheese – *"we like the peppered one best."*

- Wash and slice courgettes and cook in stock until soft (a microwave is useful). Allow to cool a little.
- Liquidize and add Boursin.
- Continue to liquidize until completely mixed.
- Taste and add salt and pepper as you wish.
- Re-heat if necessary, and serve with fresh bread.

Serves 4

Watercress soup

bunch watercress
large potato
onion
white wine (3 tabsps)
Marigold vegetable bouillon
    powder – heaped teasp
milk
clove of garlic
seasoning
25g butter

Serves 4

- Cut off the thick stalks of the washed watercress, and put aside a few sprigs.
- Chop potato and onion, and peel a garlic clove.
- Melt butter in saucepan, stew potato, onion and garlic gently for a few minutes.
- Add watercress and wine and continue to heat gently.
- Add 900ml boiling water, and heaped teaspoon of Marigold powder (or a stock cube).
- Simmer c.15-20 minutes and liquidize.
- Add a little milk, check seasoning, and garnish with the fresh chopped watercress leaves, as you serve it.

Microwave mushroom soup

6oz (150g) thinly sliced
    mushrooms
1¼ pts (750ml) chicken
    stock
1 medium onion, chopped
¼ pt (150ml) single cream
1oz (25g) margarine
salt and pepper
2 teasps cornflour
4 teasps water

- Place mushrooms, onions and margarine in a bowl and cook 2 minutes on high.
- Add stock, and cook on high for 6 minutes.
- Thicken with cornflour and the water, blended together.
- Cook 1 min. on high (may need a little longer).
- Stir in the cream.
- Liquidize and serve.

This can be prepared in advance and re-heated **slowly** and **gently** in a saucepan if more convenient. *Serves 4 - 6*

Parsnip soup

1lb (400g) parsnips or
    thereabouts.
onion
juice ½ lemon and ½ orange.
1½ pts (900ml) stock (made
    with stock cube)

- Peel and slice parsnip and chop onion.
- Put in pan with juices and c. 1½ pts stock.
- Simmer 30-45 minutes.
- Liquidize and taste. A little milk may be added to thin the soup.

Serves 4

Carrot and lentil soup

4oz (100g) red lentils
1 onion, chopped
1lb (400g) carrots, sliced
1 level teasp ground
    coriander
2pts (1.2l) stock (use 2
    stock cubes)
2 teasps lemon juice
chives

- Put everything in a large pan, simmer 1 hour, stirring occasionally.
- Purée.
- Reheat, garnish with chopped chives.

Serves 6

Bacon and chestnut soup

1 small onion
2 rashers of bacon
15g fresh sage
can of chestnut purée
400ml chicken stock
salt and pepper
crème fraiche
chopped parsley

- Sauté the onion, bacon and sage in a large saucepan until soft.
- Add chestnut purée, stock, salt and pepper and simmer for 15 minutes.
- (Optional: Serve with spoonful of crème fraiche and parsley.)

Serves 4

Vegetable soup

choose from:
    potato, carrot, swede,
    parsnip, onion, celery,
    leek, cabbage, tomato,
    broccoli
garlic
Marigold bouillon powder,
    (1 heaped teasp)
a little butter or oil
parsley
chives

Serves 4 - 6

- Boil or steam the potatoes, carrots, swede, parsnip. If boiling, use as little water as possible, and very little salt. When cooked, drain and **save** the water.
- Do the same with the broccoli, cabbage and tomato.
- Sauté in butter or oil the onion, celery, leek and garlic until soft.
- Reduce cooked vegetables to a purée in a blender. Use the cooking water to thin.
- Dissolve Marigold powder in hot water and add as necessary to achieve the consistency of a soup.
- Taste for seasoning and add pepper and salt if needed.
- Serve with fresh herbs (eg parsley, chives) on top, or sprinkle with dried herbs before final heating.

The method for this soup can be adapted to the range of vegetables to hand, the preferred balance of vegetables according to taste, and to the number to be served.

2 onions
2 leeks
2 medium potatoes
25g butter
stock cube
dried mixed or fresh herbs

"If cooking for one, eat some and save a portion for the next day. Freeze the rest."

Easy leek and potato soup

- Chop onions or slice finely and add to melted butter in saucepan.
- While the onions soften, prepare the leeks and the potatoes by cleaning and chopping.
- Add them to pan, and let them soften.
- Put in a stock cube and then add water to cover vegetables. (No need to dissolve the stock cube separately.)
- Simmer for 15 minutes or until vegetables are soft.
- For a creamy soup, purée with a hand-held blender, or alternatively mash up a few of the potato bits to thicken it slightly. For a chunky soup, serve as is.

"If served cold and blended, with some cream stirred in and topped with chives, you can call it vichyssoise. As it is pale, a little greenery, eg parsley or chives, looks good on top served hot."

Serves 4

TODAY'S RECIPE:
Easy summer fish pie

**FLAVOURS of the sea.
SERVES four to six.**

Ingredients

500g new potatoes
200g frozen peas
150g cooked prawns
300g hot smoked salmon, flaked
200ml creme fraiche
Zest and juice of 1 lemon, plus 1 lemon cut into wedges to serve
Handful of dill, chopped
20g butter
2 spring onions, sliced
Handful chives, snipped
20g Parmesan, grated

Method

1 Heat oven to 200c/180c fan/gas 6. Boil scrubbed potatoes (halve large ones) for 15 minutes or until tender. Meanwhile, put the peas in a small bowl and pour over boiling water to defrost. Leave to stand for a few minutes, then drain.

2 Tip into a large bowl and combine with the prawns, salmon, creme fraiche, lemon zest, juice and dill, seasoning well with black pepper and a little salt — the smoked fish is quite salty, so be careful not to add too much. Tip into an ovenproof dish, roughly 15 x 24cm, and spread evenly.

3 Drain the potatoes and stand for a minute, then tip back into the pan with the butter and seasoning. Crush with a fork or potato masher, skins and all. Stir through the spring onions and chives, and spoon on top of the filling. Scatter over the Parmesan and bake for 20 minutes until golden.

■ RECIPE of the day is brought to you in association with BBC Good Food Magazine. Why not subscribe today and get your first five issues for £5 (direct debit only)? Visit buysubscriptions.com/goodfood and enter code GFDAILY16 or 0844 848 3434 and quote GFDAILY16.

BBC **goodfood**

How SAT
crush th
potenti
of the ne
generati

THE branding of almost half of all
11-year-old pupils as 'failures' (Mail),
to tough new SATs tests, is nothing
the Fifties, the official measure
n was solely academic ability,
failure rate of more the

Easy variants: vegetable soup

To the onions, add a mixture of chopped carrots and celery, and proceed as above.

Alternatively fresh, left over cooked vegetables can be added, plus a tin of tomatoes, and some herbs. Add stock and proceed to cook for a shorter time, simply to re-heat the vegetables.

Easy variants: red lentil soup

2oz (50g) red lentils
2 onions
2 teasps cumin
½ teasp or 1 teasp chilli (to
    taste)
½ teasp turmeric
black pepper
25g butter
carrots and/or tin tomatoes

- Soften the onions and spices in the butter.
- Add the carrots or the tomatoes, plus stock cube and water.
- Meanwhile boil the lentils for 15 minutes and then add to the soup.

NB   Although red lentils are used, if you also add the turmeric, it ends up orange. It has been mistaken for mulligatawny!

Chicken stock

1 onion, quartered (don't bother to peel)
1 carrot – cut into 3 chunks,
1 celery stalk – cut into 3 chunks
bouquet-garni (thyme, bay leaves and a couple of sage leaves, tied together with raffia or fine kitchen string)
whole black peppercorns and salt
carcase of roast chicken

Place carcase into a heavy pan with vegetables and bouquet garni, and cover with water.

- Bring to a simmer, skim off any foam, simmer for about 30 minutes, cool rapidly.
- Strain through a fine sieve and chill until the stock sets.
- Remove any fat that sets on the top.
- Freeze in a plastic box.

"Tip: Put any remaining stock into an ice-cube bag – pour in through a funnel – you then always have small amounts of stock to add to sauces.

Do not add any skin – which would produce a lot of fat on the top of your stock, and make the stock cloudy."

Lamb / beef stock

Lamb or beef bones
1 onion, quartered (don't
   bother to peel)
1 carrot – cut into 3 chunks,
1 celery stalk – cut into 3
   chunks
tablespoon of cooking oil
bouquet-garni (thyme and
   bay leaves, tied together
   with raffia or fine kitchen
   string)
whole black peppercorns and
   salt
water / red wine

- Pre-heat a heavy based pan, add cooking oil and heat, add vegetables.
- Cook over a medium heat until the vegetables begin to soften and brown.
- Add the bones, increase heat and keep the contents of the pan on the move until bones also begin to brown.
- Add water OR red wine and water, bouquet-garni, peppercorns and salt.
- Bring the mixture to the boil.
- Cover and then turn down to a soft simmer.
- Cook very slowly for about 1 hour.
- Cool rapidly.
- Strain through a fine sieve and chill until the stock sets.
- Remove any fat that sets on the top.

"Freeze in a plastic box and put any remaining stock into an ice-cube bag – pour in through a funnel – you then always have small amounts of stock to add to sauces."

Soup as a Meal

1 large tin chicken soup
tin frankfurters
cupful of frozen peas
cupful of sweetcorn, (or small
    packet of frozen mixed
    vegetables)
2 bacon rashers (optional)

Supper standby

- Drain frankfurters and wash off any brine by running water over them in a sieve.
- Cook the frozen vegetables in salted water for a few minutes while also heating the soup. Add the vegetables to the soup, then stir in chopped frankfurters.
- If a couple of bacon rashers are to hand, fry them, snip into small pieces, and add.
- Heat through.

"Served with bread rolls for dunking, it makes quite a satisfying meal. " Serves 2

Smoky fish chowder

8oz (200g) smoked
    haddock
1 cooked potato, chopped
    very small
1 red pepper, thinly sliced
1 leek, cut into chunks
4 sticks celery, chopped
4oz (100g) frozen sweet
    corn
2 teasps flour
25g butter
white wine
chopped parsley

- Poach haddock gently, in water to cover, plus a splash of white wine, for 10 minutes. Remove fish and keep poaching liquid.
- Meanwhile, melt butter, and sauté pepper, leek and celery until soft.
- Add flour and mix well, then add poaching liquid little by little.
- Simmer for a few minutes; add fish flaked in small pieces, sweet corn and potato, and simmer for a few minutes.
- Garnish and serve.

Serves 2

Lamb bone soup

1 bone from a roast leg of
   lamb, preferably still
   with some meat
1 medium onion, sliced
   and chopped
2 medium potatoes,
   peeled and diced,
2 medium carrots, peeled
   and diced,
additional vegetables:
parsnip, peeled and sliced
   or diced, probably 1 or
   2 small
1 stick of celery, chopped,
red kidney beans, small
   tin, drained
any left over vegetables,
   cut small
1 teasp mixed herbs
salt and pepper

- Put the lamb bone and all the vegetables into a large pan and add enough boiling water to cover the bone and vegetables (probably 2pts/1 litre). Bring to the boil and simmer for at least 30 minutes or until the vegetables are soft.
- Leave to cool slightly
- Take out the lamb bone and cut the remaining meat off it and put back into the soup. Discard the bone.
- If the vegetables have been cut up very small the soup can be eaten as it is. If they are larger, or if you prefer, put the soup into a blender to make into a thick broth.

This soup freezes well. Put into plastic boxes and defrost for several hours before reheating. If you have made a very thick broth it can be diluted with boiling water or vegetable stock. This is a nourishing soup made from leftovers from a roast meal, with extra vegetables. The amount and choice of vegetables can vary according to taste and availability.

Serves 6 to 8

Jenny's easy Cawl

"Cawl is a Welsh soup which needs to be made over two days, but this version takes very little effort."

6 lamb cutlets
2 cupfuls of diced/chopped
    mainly root vegetables –
    eg chopped celery, carrot,
    parsnip, swede/turnip
    (very little), potato; **or**
frozen mixed vegetables
    would do.
1 or 2 leeks, essential
salt and peppercorns

Day 1:

- Trim off some fat and simmer cutlets in 1 pt or so water with salt and a few peppercorns for c.1 hour.
- Take out cutlets, and keep cool overnight.
- Leave stock to cool completely.

Day 2:

- Take fat off stock – it should be in a solid piece.
- Strain the stock through muslin or a coffee filter paper – not essential, but it takes out the bits.
- Put all the vegetables except the leek in the stock and simmer gently for c. 30-45 minutes. If you use frozen, allow 10 minutes, in which case forget the potato.
- Pull the lean meat off the cutlets – the main 'eyes' come easily, the rest is very tedious and can be omitted – its job has been done in the stock. Divide meat into small pieces.
- Cut up the leeks quite finely, reserving a couple of inches of the green part.
- Add leeks and meat to the dish and simmer c. 10 minutes.

To serve, sprinkle the top with really finely shredded green leek.

Serves 2 - 3

Fish

Portuguese baked fish

thickish fillet of white fish (ie
    cod / fresh haddock, not
    plaice), sufficient for two
small onion, chopped
crushed garlic clove
3 sliced tomatoes
3 tabsps white wine
olive oil
juice of half a lemon
25g breadcrumbs

- Heat olive oil in a frying pan and add chopped onion and garlic to soften.
- Add breadcrumbs, and fry till crisp.
- Add tomatoes and white wine, and heat through.
- Place the fish in a shallow cooking dish (oil it first), and season with salt and pepper.
- Spoon the mixture from the frying pan over the fish.
- Cook one shelf above centre of oven, gas 5, 190ºC/375ºF for 15-20 minutes.

Serves 2

Trout in a parcel

2 prepared trout
fennel bulb
carrot
2 shallots or small onion
butter

Serves 2

- Lay each trout on its own piece of greased foil.
- Stuff chopped fennel and carrot into their middles, add a couple of slices of lemon. Season.
- Slice shallots/onions into rings and spread over the trout. Add 1 tabsp of white wine and a knob of butter to each. Wrap up loosely, but seal tightly.
- Cook gas 4 180°C/350°F centre of oven, for 30 minutes or so.

Salmon steaks

2 salmon steaks
4 tabsps white wine
25g butter
dill/fennel/parsley

Serves 2

- Place each steak on its own piece of foil and add to each 2 tabsps white wine, a dab of butter, seasoning, and, if you have it, dill or fennel or parsley.
- Wrap loosely, seal well, bake gas 7, 210°C/425°F for 10 minutes, and check. They may need a little longer.

Creamy baked haddock and tatties

12oz (300g) smoked haddock (skinned) and broken into chunks.
1 leek, finely sliced
¼pt (150ml) double cream
2 medium baking potatoes (skins on), sliced very thinly.
handful flat leaf parsley

Serves 2

- Scatter haddock, leek and parsley over bottom of microwaveable dish. mix with fingers.
- Drizzle over half the cream and 4 tabsps water
- Layer the potatoes over the fish and the leeks, drizzle over the remaining cream and season with salt and pepper.
- Cover dish with cling film, and pierce this several times. Microwave on "high" for 10 minutes, until liquid is bubbling and potatoes are tender.
- Heat grill.
- Remove cling film and place dish under grill until potatoes are golden.
- Leave to stand for a minute before serving.

Trout with bacon

4 lean bacon rashers
2 whole trout, cleaned and filleted
3 tabsps white wine
tabsp chopped parsley

Serves 2

- Grease a small oven proof dish and cover the base with two bacon rashers.
- Put the trout on top, add pepper and parsley if you wish, then cover with the other bacon rashers.
- Add the white wine.
- Bake gas 6, 200°C/400°F for 15 minutes.

Quick fishy vegetable bake

any left-over root vegetables,
    sufficient for 4, – if
    necessary add frozen
    vegetables from your
    freezer, eg peas, beans,
    sweetcorn
frozen fish pieces for 4
4 hard boiled eggs – optional
2 tomatoes – sliced
I small bag crisps – crushed

For the **White Sauce**:
2oz (50g) butter
2oz (50g) flour
1pt (600ml) of warm milk

Serves 4

- Begin by steaming and cooling the fish.
- Melt butter in heavy based pan, add flour, beat well together, cook slowly for 2 minutes.
- Add warmed milk *bit by bit* beating thoroughly after each addition until thick, smooth and glossy.
- Butter an ovenproof dish big enough to take all the ingredients.
- Arrange vegetables evenly in the dish. Season with salt and freshly ground black pepper and if possible a handful of chopped chives, or chopped thyme in winter.
- Peel the hard boiled eggs, chop and scatter over the vegetable mixture. Add the sliced tomatoes and the flaked fish.
- Pour the sauce over the vegetable mixture. Sprinkle over the crushed crisps.
- Bake at gas 4, 180°C/350°F until the top is golden brown and the dish is obviously sizzling.

Serve with hunks of good warm bread or a salad.

Fresh mackerel fillets with mustard sauce

1 mackerel per person
a little cooking oil
1oz (25g) rolled/porridge
    oats per fish
salt and fresh pepper

For the sauce *for two*:
1 tabsp mayonnaise
1 teasp Dijon / French
    mustard

Serves 2 (double up for 4)

- Get your fish provider to gut and clean the mackerel and cut into 2 fillets.
- Wash and pat dry.
- With your hands, lightly oil the flesh and skin side of the fish.
- Place the oats on a plate; dip each oiled fillet in the oats, turn over and repeat on other side.
- Heat a non-stick pan and place the fillets in. Cook for only about 5 minutes on each side.
- Combine the ingredients for the sauce.
- Plate the fish and serve the sauce on the side.

Serve with:
Baby new potatoes and peas, or a crisp salad and sauté potatoes/oven chips,

Oven baked fish fillets with lemon mayonnaise

1 white fish fillet per person (skinned)
1oz (25g) white bread crumbs per person
chopped parsley and chives
1 egg
a little flour
2 lemons
1 tabsp mayonnaise per person

- Pre heat the oven to 180°C/350°F, gas 4.
- Beat the egg and place in a dish big enough to take a fish fillet.
- Place flour in another dish and season well with salt and pepper.
- Place the breadcrumbs in another dish and add the chopped parsley and herbs. Add the grated rind from one lemon. Season well with salt and pepper. Combine well.
- Wash and pat dry each fillet. Lightly oil a baking tray.
- Dip each fillet into the flour, then the beaten egg and then the breadcrumb mixture. Place on baking tray.
- Bake for about 15 minutes until nicely golden.
- Put mayonnaise in a small dish. Add the grated rind from the second lemon and some salt. Juice both the lemons, but only add enough to the mayonnaise mixture to make a thin sauce — *not too runny*.
- Plate the fish and serve the sauce separately

Serve with pasta or new potatoes and oven roasted tomatoes.

1 red pepper – chunked
1 red onion – cut into 8
    chunks
1 small bulb fennel – sliced
2 large firm tomatoes –
    quartered, *or* 400g can
    peeled or chopped
    tomatoes
garlic cloves – chopped
1 bay leaf
1 teasp smoked paprika
1pt (600ml) chicken/fish
    stock (plus 1 tabsp
    Pernod)
1 tabsp olive oil
salt and freshly ground
    pepper
fish – cod, salmon, frozen
    raw prawns
halved mange touts or a
    handful of frozen peas.

Portuguese fish stew

- Poach the onion, fennel, garlic and peppers in the olive oil.
- Add garlic, paprika and bay leaf.
- Add tomatoes and stock – season well.
- Simmer till vegetables are *"as you like 'em"*.
- Add fish and simmer for maximum 5 minutes.

"Serve in warm bowls with a good hunk of yummy bread, a crisp salad and some very chilled wine – Rosé is lush with this!"

NB. If using ready cooked prawns add just before you serve, don't actually *cook* them – they will become very tough of you do.

Serves 2

Haddock Monte Carlo

Smoked haddock for 2
   (preferably un-dyed)
4 tomatoes
100g long grain rice
25g butter
juice of ½ a lemon
chopped parsley

- Put rice, chopped tomatoes, lemon juice, butter, some milled pepper, 100ml of water into a 7" or 8" heavy lidded pan (eg a round Le Creuset).
- Cover and cook very gently for 10 minutes.
- Add the fish cut into a few pieces – preferably skinned, but this is not essential; use a wooden spoon to get it down below the rice, so that the fish is covered. Add some more water – try a few tabsps.
- Cook gently for 15 minutes. Watch it to see if it is sticking – and add a little more water if necessary, but it should not be too runny when cooked.

Serves 2

Poultry

Devilled drumsticks

4 chicken drum sticks
at least three of: tomato
    ketchup, mushroom
    ketchup, soy sauce, runny
    mustard, soft brown sugar,
    5ml wine vinegar
curry powder
10ml olive oil.

Serves 2

- Slash the drumsticks and put in an oiled meat tin/baking dish to cook, preferably not much bigger than the drumsticks can go in comfortably.
- Make a runny mix of any of the other ingredients you choose plus curry powder and olive oil, and turn the drumsticks round in it.
- Leave to absorb the flavours for 30 minutes if you are that well organised, otherwise just cook in a pre-heated oven gas 5, 190°C/375°Ffor about 40 minutes. They may take a bit less or more, depending on size.

Chicken parcels

2 chicken breasts with the
skin removed
2 cloves garlic, crushed
2 tabsps orange juice
2 teasps lemon
2 teasps olive oil
salt and pepper to taste

Serves 2

- Lay out a piece of foil for each breast, brush the foil with oil, and place chicken breast on top.
- Mix the other ingredients and divide equally between the two breasts, and pour over.
- Make into loose well-sealed parcels and cook for about 30-40 minutes at gas 4, 180ºC/350ºF. Stick a sharp knife in to test that the pink-ness has gone.

A variation on this is to add chopped spring onions *or* soy sauce *or* a few slices of root ginger.

Chicken with courgettes and lime

2 chicken breasts cut in small
    strips
2 teasps olive oil
soy sauce
black pepper
200g courgettes
2 limes
salt and pepper

- Put the chicken strips in a dish with the oil, soy and pepper, swish about and leave to marinade for at least an hour.
- Cut the courgettes into 'match sticks', sauté them briefly in a little oil, and remove from pan. Stir-fry the drained chicken until cooked through, pour on the juice of one lime, add the courgettes to re-heat, season and toss.
- Serve at once with lime slices for garnish.

Serves 2 – or, as a starter, 4

Jane's apricot chicken

6 chicken thighs, boned and
    skinned (much easier)
420g tin apricots
packet of Ainsley Harriott
    French Onion Soup.
a little flour
butter for frying

*"Easy and delicious for dinner
with friends (or in a caravan)."*

- Flour thighs and brown in butter. Place in a casserole dish.
- Liquidize the apricots and pour over the chicken.
- Scatter dried soup mixture over everything, cover, and pop in oven, gas 5, 190°C/375°F for 30-45 minutes.
- If wished, add a small amount of garlic and herbs when browning the chicken.

Serves 3

32

Chicken and spring vegetable stir-fry

1 rounded teasp cornflour

1½ tabsps of light soy sauce

1 small clove of garlic, peeled and crushed

1 small piece of ginger, peeled and grated

1 small red chilli, de-seeded and finely chopped

2 skinless chicken breasts, chopped into small pieces

1 tabsp groundnut or other flavourless oil

6 spring onions, sliced

1½oz (40g) cashew nuts

1 small head broccoli florets, stem sliced into thin rounds

½ pointed cabbage, tough stalk removed and finely sliced

flavourless oil

- In a bowl, mix cornflour, soy sauce, garlic, ginger, and chilli.
- Add chicken and stir well.
- Heat ½ tabsp oil in non-stick wok and add cashew nuts; stir fry until brown, remove and **drain** on kitchen paper. Increase heat and add chicken mixture to wok for 3-4 minutes – continue to stir fry until golden, then remove to a bowl.
- Add remaining oil to wok, then spring onions, broccoli and cabbage and stir fry.
- Add 2 tabsp water and remaining soy sauce, and cook for a further 2 minutes until vegetables are steamed and very nearly tender.
- Return chicken and nuts to wok and continue to stir-fry until chicken is cooked through.

Serves 2

"Slim" chicken

Serves 2 – can easily double for 4; just use 8 thighs and 2 tins of tomatoes.

4 chicken thighs
1 onion – finely chopped
2 cloves garlic – finely
    chopped
8 basil leaves
1 teasp chicken Bovril in 2
    tablespoons hot water
or use 2 tabsps home made
    chicken stock
210g can chopped tomatoes
4 mushrooms – cleaned
salt and freshly ground black
    pepper
olive oil and sugar

- Bone and skin the chicken thighs (or buy pre-prepared). Put on chopping board, cover with cling film and "batter out" using small side of meat mallet or a rolling pin. Don't make them wafer thin!!
- Put olive oil into a sauté pan and warm, add the chopped onion and cook until softened and just starting to colour.
- Add the garlic and cook for 2 minutes over a medium heat. *Do not burn the garlic.*
- Remove onion and garlic from pan and allow to cool. Season each chicken piece with salt and pepper, and divide the onion and garlic mixture equally over the pieces.
- Add 2 basil leaves and roll up.
- Secure with a cocktail stick.
- Add a little olive oil to sauté pan and warm. Remove stalks from the mushrooms and then quarter the heads. Add stalks and mushroom quarters to the pan, season and fry over high heat for 2 minutes.
- Remove from pan and set aside. Add the prepared chicken rolls and sear evenly. Add the mushrooms, the chicken stock and the tinned tomatoes. Check the

seasoning and add a little sugar – improves the flavour of the tomatoes.

- Cover and either simmer gently for 15 minutes or place in moderate oven, gas 4, 180°C/350°F, until chicken is just cooked through.
- Serve with pasta: cook pasta in plenty of salted water, drain *reserving* 2 tablespoons of the water. Put pasta back in pan with reserved water, then toss in a good handful of chopped basil, chives or whatever fresh herbs you like. Shake well.

- Serve immediately with a crisp green salad.
- To make this dish slim-line, use a granulated sweetener instead of sugar and a low calorie spray instead of the olive oil.

Healthy quick chicken curry

4 chicken breasts
2 teasps mild curry powder
2 handfuls raisins
2 handfuls peas (frozen)
2 cups rice
oil
3 tabsps goats' milk yoghurt

- Chop chicken into small pieces and stir-fry in large pan.
- Add raisins and peas, stir in curry powder and season with salt and pepper.
- Heat thoroughly.
- Finally, add yoghurt and serve with boiled rice.

"My children's favourite"   *Serves 4*

2 tabsp Madras curry paste
(If you prefer a milder
curry use a Korma paste)
4 skinless, boneless chicken
breasts, cut into 3cm
pieces
1 medium onion, sliced
210g can chopped tomatoes
200ml chicken stock
120g Philadelphia soft
cheese
50g blanched flaked almonds
50g sultanas

Creamy chicken curry

- Heat a large non-stick saucepan and add the curry paste, chicken pieces and onion.
- Fry gently for 5-6 minutes.
- Stir in the tomatoes,chicken stock, almonds and sultanas.
- Bring to the boil. Cover and simmer gently for 15 minutes until the chicken is tender.
- Remove the pan from the heat and stir in the Philadelphia cheese until melted.

Serve with basmati rice.

Serves 4

Susie's coronation chicken

1 large cooked chicken
2 tabsps oil
1 large onion
3-4 tabsps medium or hot
    curry powder
1 teasp tomato paste
juice of ½ lemon
2 heaped tabsps mango
    chutney
¼pt (150ml) chicken stock
mayonnaise

- Fry onion in oil to soften. Add curry powder and cook for a few minutes, then add tomato paste, chutney, stock and lemon juice.
- Simmer for 10 minutes.
- Strain and cool (the sauce can be frozen at this stage).
- Add small amounts of sauce to mayonnaise, according to how strong you want it. How much mayonnaise depends on size of chicken.
- Strip the cooked meat from the chicken carcase, chop into small pieces, and stir them into the sauce.

Serves 8

Quick stuffed peppers with turkey

2 peppers –1 red, 1 orange
300g minced fresh turkey
1 onion – finely chopped
garlic – finely chopped, as
    you want
½ teasp dried mixed herbs
or 1 teasp chopped fresh
    chives, thyme, sage
salt and freshly ground black
    pepper
Fry Light
red chilli – chopped and de-
    seeded (for an extra zing)

- Heat oven to gas 4, 180°C/350°F.
- Spray a frying pan with Fry Light and cook the onion until soft and golden but **not** brown. Add the garlic and cook for about 3 minutes over a moderate heat. Remove from the heat and cool.
- Meanwhile clean, halve and deseed the peppers. Dry thoroughly.
- In a large bowl, combine the minced turkey, onion, garlic and herbs, and season well with salt and freshly ground black pepper; using your hands (dampen under cold water) make into 4 balls. Push into the pepper halves.
- Put the peppers on a non-stick tray and bake in oven for about 35/40 minutes till nicely golden on the tops.
- Serve with creamy mash, or steamed vegetables, or pasta or couscous.

Serves 2 – easily doubles/trebles

Beef

Amazing beef burgers
(an easy recipe with one bowl)

1lb (400g) good lean beef,
    minced
1 large red onion
2 eggs
1 tabsp Worcestershire sauce
2 tabsps tomato ketchup
handful flour
salt/pepper
spoonful oregano

- Chop onion small.
- Put all ingredients into a bowl, and squash together with your hands.
- Make burger patties the size you like to eat.
- Place on oven tray in pre-heated oven at 180°C/350°F, gas 4, and cook until brown (30 minutes).

Stifado – Greek beef stew

4lbs (1.6kg) braising steak
⅔ cup cooking oil
1 can (6oz) tomato paste
1½ cups red wine
8 peppercorns
2 bay leaves
1½ tabsps ground all-spice
2 garlic cloves, halved
5 whole cloves
salt and pepper to taste
1lb (400g) small onions

- Use a large lidded pan.
- Cut the meat into 1" squares and sauté it in oil until brown.
- Add all the ingredients except onions.
- Bring to a quick boil, cover, and simmer gently for 1 hr. Add more wine if necessary.
- Add the onions and cook until tender, another 30-40 minutes.
- Discard the garlic and cloves. Taste for seasoning.

The final mixture should be thick.

Serves 12 – "ideal for a buffet"

This dish may also be prepared beforehand and kept for 1 to 2 days in the fridge, or it can be frozen. Thaw at room temperature and reheat.

Smothered steak

6oz (150g) braising steak in
    one piece, per person
    x 4
340g tin sweet corn
butter
2 onions
6oz (150g) mushrooms
Oxo stock cube

- Soften onions in butter, plus mushrooms and sweet corn.
- Season and blend in flour plus Oxo stock.
- Put meat in a casserole and cover with sauce.
- Cook 3 hours at gas mark 2, 150°C/300°F.

Jacket potatoes and green salad make good accompaniments. *Serves 4*

Peggy's steak, bacon and sage pie

500g braising steak
8 unsmoked back bacon
    rashers
handful sage leaves, roughly
    chopped
cooking oil
500ml chicken stock
puff pastry

Serves 4-6

- Slice beef into 3cm squares and the bacon rashers into 3cm wide strips.
- Brown the steak and bacon in a saucepan in oil, and add chicken stock. Season with pepper.
- Simmer gently until the beef is tender, c. 1 hr – check.
- Put into a pie dish, and cover with puff pastry (follow the instructions on the packet for rolling out the pastry).
- Bake in oven at gas mark 4, 180°C/350°F for approx. 40 minutes.

Di's basic beef casserole

1lb (400g) casserole steak
2 large onions
2 carrots
6oz (100g) mushrooms
tin tomatoes
red wine
tomato paste
flour
beef stock cube
thyme, bay leaf, or mixed herbs

- Soften onions in a large lidded pan.
- Chop beef into bite sized pieces, and toss them in flour (some people use a see-through poly bag for this).
- Add beef to pan and brown.
- Chop vegetables and add to pan.
- Add stock cube, tomato purée, herbs, then water to cover.
- Bring to boil, then simmer **very** slowly on top of stove, or cook in an oven at gas mark 2, 160°C/300°F for 2½ - 3 hours.

Basic beef casserole variation: Beef in red wine

Follow steps 1-3 above, then add ½ bottle of red wine, herbs (thyme, rosemary, bay leaf), tomato purée, mushrooms, and any other vegetables desired. Bring to the simmer and cook very gently as above.

Microwaved beef stroganoff

1kg (2lb) rump steak (cut into 2"x½" strips)
50g (2oz) plain flour
salt & pepper to taste
1 large onion – finely chopped
30ml (2 tabsps) tomato purée
450ml (¾pt) hot beef stock, eg Oxo cube
150ml (¼ pt) red wine
100g (4oz) mushrooms, sliced
300ml (½ pt) soured cream

Serves 4

- Toss the steak with the flour, salt & pepper until it is evenly coated. *("We sift the flour first to make it easier.")*
- Place the steak, remaining flour, onion, tomato purée, beef stock and red wine in a casserole dish, with ample room to spare.
- Cover and cook on **medium** for 45 minutes (yes, this long, says our contributor).
- Stir in the mushrooms and soured cream.
- Cook on **medium** for a further 5 to 10 minutes.
- Stir thoroughly.

A casserole suitable for a microwave is essential. The recipe is from a cookery-book for an 850 watt microwave so it might overflow in a more powerful oven.

Reheats well (in the microwave) the following day; best to use "low" setting.

Cornish pasty pie

A variation on the traditional Cornish Pasty. In the 18th Century, Cornish tin miners' wives would cook a pasty for their husbands, wrap it in a cloth and take it to the mine at midday. They were eaten in the hand, hot or cold. "*This recipe is quite as delicious, without all the trouble of making individual pasties.*"

For the pastry:
1lb (400g) all purpose
    flour
½lb (200g) butter or
    margarine
enough water to mix.

For the filling:
1¼lbs (500g) chuck
    (braising) steak
¼-½lb (100-200g) ox
    kidney (optional)
1 medium turnip
1 large onion
1 large potato
½ teasp mixed herbs
1 tabsp water
pepper & salt to taste

- Rub the fat into the flour until it resembles breadcrumbs. Add enough water to mix to a firm dough and leave to rest.
- Cut the steak and the kidney into bite size pieces.
- Peel and dice the turnip and the onion, mix in a large bowl with the steak and kidney. Peel the potato, cut it into thin slices.
- Roll out half the pastry, large enough to line a 10" loose bottom flan tin with about ½" overlapping. Line the base of the pastry with the potato, then add all the other ingredients. Roll out the remaining pastry to cover the pie, damping the edges to seal well. Pierce top in 2 or 3 places.
- Place the pie in a preheated oven and cook at gas mark 5, 190°C/375°F for 20 minutes, then turn the oven down to mark 3, 160°C/325°F and cook for a further 1½ hours.
- When cooked, remove from the oven and allow to rest for 5 minutes before cutting into portions.

Serve on its own or with a green salad.   *Serve 4 - 6*

Basic recipe:
12oz (350g) corned beef
3oz (75g) fat
8–10oz (200g) boiled
    potatoes, sliced
2 medium size onions, finely
    chopped

Embellishment:
small tin of chopped
    tomatoes
small tin of sliced mushrooms
    and/or
small tin of sweetcorn
pinch of mixed herbs

Corned beef hash

- Boil the potatoes and then slice.
- Dice but do not flake the corned beef, and place in a bowl.
- Heat ⅔ of the fat in the pan, add the sliced potatoes and brown gently for about 5 minutes, do not mash.
- Add to the beef.
- Heat the remaining fat and fry the onions for 5 minutes, add to the corned beef and potato mixture, add salt and pepper.
- Return this mixture to the pan and heat thoroughly.

It can be embellished with tomatoes, sliced mushrooms and/or sweetcorn and a pinch of mixed herbs before the final heating of the mixture.

Serves 2 to 3, or 4 with green vegetables alongside.

Lamb / Pork

Creamy lamb casserole

10oz (250g) lamb fillet
6-8oz (150-200g) onions
6-8oz (150-200g) carrots
tin drained butter beans
stock (use Swiss Marigold
    powder)
seasoning

- Slice lamb about ¾" thick and coat liberally with seasoned flour.
- Fry lamb on fairly high heat until lightly browned.
- Fry onions and carrot until onions soften.
- Put all the above into a casserole, add the butter beans and cover with the hot stock (but not too much – you can always add more).
- Put the lid on the casserole and cook in oven on gas mark 2, 150°C/300°F, for about 1½ hours.

Serves 3

Moroccan lamb

1lb (400g) lamb in bite sized
    chunks, tossed in flour
2 large onions, chopped
2 carrots, chopped
2 sticks celery, chopped
½lb (200g) mushrooms
1 tin chopped tomatoes and
    tomato purée
4 oz (100g) dried ready-to-eat
    apricots
1" piece of root ginger,
    chopped very small
1 teasp cumin
cinnamon and nutmeg to taste
1 bay leaf
mixed herbs
stock cube

- Soften onions in oil, with ginger and spices, vegetables and herbs.
- Add floured lamb.
- Add stock cube and water to cover.
- Bring to boil, then transfer to oven on gas mark 3, 170°C/325°F for 2 hours (or simmer very gently on top of stove).
- Add apricots, and cook for a further ½ hour.

Serve with couscous, or brown rice, with lots of fresh chopped mint, a squeeze of lemon and yoghurt. Lime wedges for garnish if desired.

Serves 4

1lb (400g) minced lamb/beef
tomato ketchup
potatoes
1 aubergine
tin chopped tomatoes
packet cheese sauce
grated cheese

Serves 4

Beverley's moussaka

- Brown the meat and add a shake of tomato ketchup.
- Stir about, transfer to an oven proof dish and keep warm.
- Slice some potatoes, enough to put a layer over the meat in the dish, and deep fry. Place over the meat.
- Shallow fry some sliced aubergine, add the tin of chopped tomatoes. Layer over the potatoes.
- Make up a packet of cheese sauce according to instructions and put over.
- Finish with a sprinkling of grated cheese and cook in oven on gas mark 4, 180°C/350°F for 30 minutes.

"NB Particularly enjoyed by teenagers, as a nice, warm, filling, supper. "

Cider baked pork chops

4 pork chops
4oz (100g) mushrooms,
 sliced
2 cooking apples, peeled
1 onion, sliced
salt and pepper to taste
½pt (300ml) cider
2oz (50g) breadcrumbs
4oz (100g) cheddar cheese,
 grated
watercress (optional)

- Pre-heat oven at gas mark 6, 200ºC/400ºF.
- Grease a 3pt oven-proof dish.
- Place mushrooms, apples and onions in base of dish.
- Season and lay chops on the bed of vegetables, cover with cider.
- Mix breadcrumbs and grated cheese and sprinkle over the chops.
- Bake for 1 hour until chops are thoroughly cooked and the topping is a golden colour.

Garnish with watercress and serve hot.   *Serves 4*

Pork tenderloin with apricots, stuffing and bacon

1 tenderloin
8 dried, ready-to-eat apricots
50g stuffing
4 rashers of streaky bacon

Serves 2

- Make a cut in the tenderloin length wise, sufficient to open it flat.
- Lay apricots and stuffing on top, and close tenderloin.
- Wrap streaky bacon all around.
- Bake in oven for approx. 1 hour on gas mark 4; 180ºC/350ºF.

Good to eat hot or cold.

Pork in potatoes

4 large potatoes
1 large onion
3 boneless pork chops
100ml white wine
2 crushed cloves of garlic
juniper berries
parsley if possible
seasoning

- Peel and slice potatoes and onion thinly.
- Cut off some of the fat from the chops and brown on each side in a frying pan with a little oil, and the garlic.
- Grease a casserole dish and layer in half the potatoes and onion, mixing in some chopped parsley and a few juniper berries. Season with salt and pepper.
- Place the chops and garlic on top, then the remainder of the onion and potatoes, and season again.
- Pour over the wine and 50ml hot water.
- Cover with a double sheet of greaseproof paper, then a lid and cook gas mark 1, 140°C/275°F for about 3 hours. Watch that the liquid doesn't dry out.
- Sprinkle with remaining chopped parsley.

Serves 3

Fillet of pork Basil Brush

1½lb (600g) pork fillet cut
    into ½" pieces
4 tabsps olive oil
1 small chopped onion
½ teasp basil
½ teasp sage
⅛ tabsp dill weed
flour
6 tabsps Tawny Port
½pt (300ml) beef bouillon

Serves 4

- Heat olive oil in large frying pan; add onion, herbs and ⅓ port.
- Cook until onions are soft, remove solids to casserole dish.
- Fry pork lightly all over, and put in casserole.
- Add flour to frying pan to absorb olive oil, then add bouillon slowly to cream consistency. Add ⅓ port.
- Pour into casserole and bring to boil.
- Put into slow oven gas mark 3, 170°C/325°F, until cooked, about 1½ hrs.
- Add last ⅓ port before serving or reheating.

Can be frozen.

Bacon and Sausage

4 rashers back bacon, fat removed
2oz (50g) grated cheddar cheese
small onion, chopped

[Swper Mam is Welsh for Mum's Supper[

Swper Mam

- Grease a shallow fireproof dish and lay two rashers on the base.
- Cover the rashers with chopped onion, then the cheese.
- Lay 2 rashers on top
- Bake gas 4, 180°C/350°F for c.30 minutes – check after 20 minutes.

A baked potato and green salad go excellently with this dish.

Serves 1 hearty eater or two small appetites.

Cheesy bacon and vegetable bake

Any leftover root vegetables *or* frozen vegetables eg peas, beans, sweetcorn (enough for 4)
4 bacon rashers – chopped, fried and cooled
1pt (600ml) cheese sauce
2oz (50g) grated cheese
2 hard boiled eggs – optional
2 tomatoes – sliced
1 small bag crisps – crushed

For the **cheese sauce***:*
2oz (50g) butter
2oz (50g) flour
1pt (600ml) warm milk
2oz (50g) grated cheese

Serves 4

- Melt butter in heavy based pan, add flour and beat well together.
- Allow to cook slowly for a couple of minutes.
- Add warmed milk **bit by bit** beating thoroughly after each addition.
- Gradually add the 2oz (50g) grated cheese, and beat well; it should be thick, smooth and glossy.
- Butter an ovenproof dish big enough to take all your vegetables and arrange them evenly.
- Season with salt and freshly ground black pepper. Add as many chopped chives (summer), or as much thyme (winter) as you like, followed by the sliced tomatoes. Scatter the cooked bacon pieces and chopped hard boiled eggs over the dish.
- Pour the sauce over the mixture. Sprinkle on the grated cheese and then the crushed crisps.
- Bake at gas 4, 180°C/350°F until the top is golden brown and the dish is obviously sizzling.
- Serve with hunks of good warm bread or a salad.

Quick sausage casserole for hungry children (+ adults!)

6 sausages
1 medium onion
2 cloves of garlic
5-6 closed cup mushrooms,
    chopped
handful of chopped peppers
1 tin of chopped tomatoes
1 dessertspoon of tomato
    purée
Worcestershire sauce
1 tablespoon of tomato
    ketchup
1-2 tablespoons vegetable
    stock

Serves 2 children + 2 adults

- Grill the sausages.
- Dice the onion and garlic and gently fry until soft.
- Add mushrooms and peppers and fry.
- Add tomatoes, tomato purée, a splash of Worcestershire sauce, and tomato ketchup.
- Add vegetable stock (or boiling water) until casserole reaches a pleasing consistency (not too watery or when you wrap it in the tortillas they will leak!).
- Chop the grilled sausages into 4-5 pieces each and add to the tomato sauce.
- Season to taste.

To be served with brown rice or soft flour tortillas.

"This recipe takes less than 30 minutes from fridge to table, and costs less than £5. The best sausages to use are ones with 80% meat or more, as they are the fullest in flavour."

Granny's bean and bacon pie (for Mondays)

cooked runner beans,
enough for two (left
over from Sunday
lunch
6 bacon rashers
3-4 sliced tomatoes (or
see note in italics)
sliced onion

Serves 2

- Fry onion and bacon rashers in a pan.
- Layer the bacon and onion with the beans in an oven proof dish.
- Heat the tomatoes in the pan in which the bacon and onion was cooked and pour over the layered bacon and beans in the dish.
- Cook in the oven (gas 4,180°C/350°F) for about 20 minutes.
- Eat with fresh, ideally crusty, bread.

"Useful recipe if you grow your own and have a glut of runner beans and tomatoes. If you have no fresh tomatoes, tinned will do, or a pasta type tomato sauce."

Pasta

Quick fish pasta bake

185g can tuna in brine (or salmon or any left over white fish)

cooked pasta shells for 2 people

250g can chopped tomatoes with garlic and herbs

1 small tub ready made cheese sauce (or white sauce if you don't want too much cheese)

1oz (25g) grated parmesan cheese

- Butter an ovenproof dish.
- In a bowl, combine the drained tuna, pasta shells, canned tomatoes and the ready made sauce. Season well with salt and black pepper.
- Pour into oven proof dish. Sprinkle over the Parmesan.
- Bake in hot oven (gas 6, 200°C/400°F) for 25 minutes.

Serve with a crisp green salad and, if wished, a *chilled* red / rosé wine.

Serves 2

Tuna pasta

200g pasta
tabsp olive oil
½ green pepper, thinly sliced
1 small onion, sliced
400g can tomatoes
1 courgette, chopped
1 teasp sugar
185g can tuna, drained
tabsp dried basil
2 tabsps of parmesan cheese
    (optional)

- Add pasta to large pan of boiling water, boil, uncovered until just tender. Drain.
- Heat oil in pan, add pepper and onion, cook, stirring, until vegetables are tender.
- Stir in tomatoes, courgette and sugar, simmer, uncovered until courgette is just tender.
- Add tuna and basil, stir gently until heated through.
- Serve sauce with pasta.

Can be sprinkled with 2 tabsps of parmesan cheese.

Serves 2 to 3

Penne Arabiatta

"This is a version of a dish first tasted in Tuscany, many years ago. It takes about 30 minutes from start to table."

1 tabsp olive oil
110g/4oz lardons/bacon,
   chopped
175g/6oz shallots, peeled
   and thinly sliced
175g/6oz mushrooms,
   chopped (not too small)
½ teasp dried crushed
   chillies
110g/4oz walnuts, chopped
400g tin chopped tomatoes
400g/14oz penne pasta
grated parmesan cheese

Serves 4

- Heat the oil in a pan, add the lardons/bacon and cook for 5 minutes. Add the chillies, cook for another two minutes then add the shallots, cook for a further 5 minutes, add the mushrooms and cook for 5 minutes.
- Finally add the chopped tomatoes and walnuts, bring to the boil, then reduce heat to simmering and cook for about 10 minutes until the sauce has a thick consistency. No seasoning is necessary as the lardons/bacon are usually salty enough.
- While the sauce is cooking, cook the penne until it is *al dente*, following the instructions on the packet.
- When the penne is cooked, drain it and add it to the sauce, mixing thoroughly until fully coated.

Serve with parmesan cheese grated fine, and a dressed green salad.

Photographs of some of our contributors …

… people who cook …

… share recipes …

… that work …

… and enjoy life too.

Tomato & bacon spaghetti with mushrooms

2 cloves garlic, crushed or
    1 teasp minced garlic
1 onion, peeled & finely
    chopped
2 x 400g tins chopped
    tomatoes
2 – 4 tabsps extra virgin olive
    oil
1 teasp dried (2 teasp fresh)
    oregano
1 teasp caster sugar
12oz (300g) smoked bacon -
    fat removed – diced
4oz (110g) button
    mushrooms – quartered
3oz (75g) crème fraiche /
    mascarpone cheese
8-12oz (200-300g) spaghetti
salt & pepper to taste

- In a large pan, sauté the onions in the oil for a few minutes, but do not allow to brown.
- Add extra oil (if needed) & then the garlic followed by the tomatoes, oregano & sugar.
- Bring to the boil & simmer gently, uncovered, for 10 minutes.
- Add the chopped bacon (& mushrooms if using) & simmer for a further 5 minutes.
- Stir in the crème fraiche / mascarpone cheese.
- Gently heat through & check seasoning.
- Serve with the cooked spaghetti.
- Garnish with fresh basil if available.

If prepared the day before, add the crème fraiche / mascarpone cheese on the day it's to be eaten.

Serves 4

Vegetarian

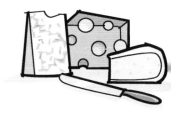

John Noakes' pie from *Blue Peter*
"A great family favourite with or without sausages"

1lb (400g) potatoes, peeled and chopped into cubes.
4 tomatoes, chopped
tabsp chopped parsley
3oz (75g) grated cheddar cheese
½pt (300ml) warmed milk or water
2ox (50g) additional grated cheese

- Put together all the dry ingredients and place in buttered pie dish.
- Pour in the liquid and cover with foil.
- Bake 1 hr at gas 4, 180ºC/350ºF
- Take out of oven, remove foil and cover the top with more grated cheese.
- Put in oven again until the top is nicely brown.

Serves 4

Mini/full size pizzas.

Uses a scone base with added herbs and black pepper.

8oz (200g) self raising flour
pinch salt
good pinch or two of herbs
2 pinches black pepper
2oz (50g) margarine
¼pt (150ml) milk
4-6oz (100-150g) grated
    cheese
1 tin chopped tomatoes

Choice of toppings – eg:
ham and pineapple chunks
bacon
pepperoni and green peppers
ham and mushroom.

- Heat oven, gas mark 7, 220°C/425°F
- Grease baking tray
- Mix, flour, salt and rub in margarine, lightly and evenly.
- Add milk in one go with herbs and pepper.
- Mix to a soft dough with a knife.
- Knead lightly on a floured surface and roll out to 5mm thickness. Cut to size as wished.
- Strain juice from tomatoes, add choice of toppings, finishing with cheese
- Bake for 15-20 minutes until golden/brown. (Base is hollow when tapped.)

Cheese savoury slice

4oz (100g) grated cheese
5oz (125g) rolled oats
2oz (50g) margarine
1 egg
½ green pepper
1 small onion
2 large carrots, grated
seasoning and herbs

- Melt the margarine and mix in the cheese, pepper, onion and carrots.
- Add the remaining ingredients
- Spread on a baking sheet and cook at gas 5, 190ºC/375ºF for 20 minutes.

This can also be used as a filling for vegetarian 'sausage' rolls. *Serves 3-4*

Survival supper

2 onions
garlic clove(s) to taste
6 boiled potatoes, medium
2 tomatoes
100g grated cheese

- Fry some onions with the garlic until brown.
- Mash up the potatoes.
- In an oven dish, layer potato and onion and grated cheese, ending with cheese.
- Add the sliced tomatoes.
- Cook gas 5, 190ºC/375ºF in oven for around 20 minutes until hot and golden brown on top.

Serves 2

Gnocchi with spinach and sage

2 x 350g packs chilled potato
    gnocchi
a few fresh sage sprigs
2 tabsps olive oil
225 (8oz) baby spinach
    leaves
200ml tub crème fraiche
1 garlic clove, crushed
75g (3oz) Vignotte cheese or
    creamy goats' cheese,
    crumbled
25g (1oz) parmesan cheese,
    finely grated

Serves 6

- Pre-heat oven to gas mark 5, 190°C/375°F (170°C fan).
- Cook gnocchi in boiling water with a few sage sprigs until the gnocchi rise to the surface.
- Drain and set aside to cool.
- Heat 1 tabsp olive oil in a frying pan and add half the spinach leaves with plenty of seasoning. Stir-fry for 1-2 minutes until wilted. Set aside and do the same with the other half.
- Stir the gnocchi and the spinach together, then spoon into an oven proof dish.
- Beat together the crème fraiche, goat's cheese and the garlic, and spoon over the gnocchi and spinach.
- Sprinkle the parmesan cheese on top.
- Cook for 20-25 minutes, when it should be piping hot.

1 good sized onion,
    coarsely chopped
2 or 3 cloves of garlic
300g (12oz) fresh gnocchi
    dumplings, (available
    from Tesco)
150g (6oz) mushrooms,
    sliced
125g (4oz) frozen peas

Serves 2

Cheddar cheese
tomato
small onion
milk
a little mustard if wished
bread slices

Quick gnocchi meal

- Sauté the onions, mushrooms and garlic in olive oil in a large frying pan. Cook until soft.
- When nearly ready, cook the gnocchi dumplings in a saucepan of boiling water for 2 minutes. They will be cooked once they start rising to the surface of the pan. Drain once cooked.
- Ditto with the peas.
- When the onions and mushrooms are cooked sufficiently, add the gnocchi dumplings and the peas to the pan and heat thoroughly; season to taste.

Increase quantities in proportion for more servings.

Tasty savoury snack

- Heat all the ingredients (except bread) in a bowl in the micro.
- Toast as many slices of bread as needed for the quantity of the other ingredients.
- Place on serving plate(s) and pour the cheese mixture over.

"Useful for using up odds and ends. Make your own variations."

Provençal crumble

1lb (400g) fresh tomatoes (or more)
1 shallot
1 tabsp olive oil
1 tabsp tomato purée
spoonful of thyme
2oz (50g) black olives
1 tabsp grated cheese.

Topping:
3oz (75g) margarine
3oz (75g) breadcrumbs
3oz (75g) flour

- Chop tomatoes, shallot, and olives.
- Heat a frying pan and sweat shallot in olive oil.
- Add all the other ingredients and place in a large, shallow heat-proof dish.
- For the topping, rub together the margarine and flour and mix in the breadcrumbs.
- Spread very thinly over the top of the tomato mixture.
- Place under grill, not too close, and allow to heat through to cook crumble until the top browns.

Serves 4 with salad

"A summer recipe for when you have a glut of tomatoes."

Mrs Beeton's cheese pudding

4oz (100g) cheddar
cheese
2 eggs
pinch cayenne pepper (or
teasp mustard)
pepper
salt
½pint (300ml) milk
1oz (25g) fresh
breadcrumbs

Serves 2

- Beat eggs slightly and add to grated cheese, mustard and seasoning.
- Boil milk, pour over mixture, then into a buttered pie-dish.
- Bake for 25-30 minutes or until raised and brown-ish.

"This is very quick, uses fridge items and is as tasty as you wish. Serve with new potatoes or chips, ratatouille, or peas, or salad. Garnish if you wish with anchovies, prawns, parsley, or parmesan."

Chilli sin carne

1 tin kidney beans in chilli
sauce
1 tin tomatoes
2 large carrots, chopped
2 large onions

Serves 2

- Soften the onions in a little oil.
- Add the vegetables, herbs, tinned beans and tinned tomatoes, and stir until simmering.
- Heat until cooked through, about 10-15 minutes.

"Add other vegetables if wished; chopped cooked potatoes mean no need to serve rice."

Gratin Dauphinois

"Although a little time-consuming to make, once this dish is in the oven you can forget about it. I make different versions of this recipe and have recently discovered a lower fat version using stock and crème fraiche as an alternative to the single cream."

25g (1oz) butter
1kg (2lb) potatoes, peeled
   and thinly sliced
1 large onion peeled and
   thinly sliced
100g (4oz) cheddar cheese
salt and pepper
150ml (¼ pint) single cream
   (milk can be used
   instead)
Use different vegetables;
eg leeks instead of onions,
or include sweet potato,
celeriac or parsnip in the
layers. No need to worry
about precise quantities.

- Butter the inside of a large casserole dish. Put a layer of potato slices, overlapping in the bottom of the casserole, dot with butter and sprinkle with onion and cheese with salt and pepper to taste.
- Pour over about one quarter of the cream. Continue with these layers until all the ingredients are used up, finishing with a layer of cheese and pouring the remaining cream on the top.
- Cover with a lid or buttered foil and bake in a moderate oven gas mark 5, 180°C/350F°, for 1 hour, removing the lid for the last 20 minutes so that the potatoes brown on the top.

Serves 4

Vegetables

2 bunches of carrots
25g butter
½ teasp sugar
½ teasp salt
1 tabsp chopped parsley
3 tabsps chopped onion
1 tabsp cream

Waterless carrots

- Peel or scrape carrots and slice them in long, thin strips.
- Sauté the onion in a little butter in a heavy saucepan, and add carrots, butter, sugar, salt, and parsley.
- Cover the pan closely, and simmer the carrots very gently on top of the stove for about 20 minutes, or place them in the oven, gas 4, 350°F/180°C, until they are done.
- Add the cream and cook about 2 minutes longer.

Roast vegetables with rosemary

2 parsnips
2 carrots
1 courgette
1 red onion
2 garlic cloves
2 sprigs rosemary
4 tabsps olive oil

- Cut vegetables in chunks and slice the garlic thinly.
- Heat oven to gas 6, 200°C/400°F. When heated pour olive oil on to a strong metal oven tray (or grill pan without rack) and heat in oven for 5 minutes.
- Add the vegetables, garlic and rosemary and turn them about to coat them in the olive oil.
- Roast for 35-40 minutes.   *Serves 3-4*

Janssen's Temptation

400g potatoes
2 onions
50g tin of anchovy fillets
black pepper
butter
½ cup cream.

- Peel and slice potatoes into wafer thin slices.
- Chop onions finely.
- Cut anchovy fillets into inch long slices.
- Butter sides of oven proof dish.
- Place layer of potatoes, then onions and top with pieces of anchovy and plenty of black pepper.
- Repeat layers until casserole is full.
- Put a few pats of butter on top; pour over the cream.
- Bake in a hot oven for 1¾ hours and serve piping hot.

A very useful side dish, which can also be offered as a main dish for 2.

Ways with mashed potatoes

Combine with finely chopped spring onions. Form into little cakes. Freeze.

Or Once combined, dip into flour and then beaten egg. Fry quickly in vegetable oil.

Or Combine with grated cheese and fried onions, dip into flour and then beaten egg. Fry quickly in vegetable oil.

Or Once combined with spring onions, add a small tin of drained crab meat, a little red Thai curry paste, salt and pepper, dip into flour and then beaten egg. Fry quickly in vegetable oil, and serve with crisp salad leaves and noodles and Oyster or Chilli dipping sauce.

Or Combine with other mashed root vegetables (swede, turnip, parsnip), add 1 beaten egg. Fill into a ring form, brush with olive oil. Bake in a very hot oven 15 minutes.

Or Add seasoning, beaten egg. Put into a piping bag (if you don't have one, make one easily from baking parchment (but *not* grease-proof paper). Just make a large icing bag and snip off the bottom]. Pipe onto an oiled baking tray and bake in hot oven until **a)** lightly golden if you want to cool and freeze or **b)** good golden colour. Eat with chops/steaks or any other meats or fish.

Or If you don't want the effort of making a piping bag, spoon into rough lumps on the oiled baking tray and cook as above.

Or Mix with beaten egg and then freeze complete in a box or plastic bag. Freeze. Once thawed use to top savoury pies.

Or Mix with cooked flaked fish (salmon, white fish, tinned sardines or tuna) lots of chopped parsley. Season well. Using damp hands, form into little cakes. Fry quickly in vegetable oil.

70

Ways with cooked baby new potatoes

Chop into smallish bits, add chopped parsley and enough olive oil to make a stiff mixture. Oil a baking tray. Fill ring forms with the potato mixture and bake until lightly golden, or chill quickly and freeze. Season well with sea salt and serve whilst still good and crisp. They go well with meat or fish.

Or

Chop into small pieces. In a small omelette pan, cook a chopped spring onion and soften for just a couple of minutes. (Add finely chopped bacon if you have some to use up.) Add the chopped potatoes and season well. Add 2 well beaten eggs and cook gently until the egg begins to set on the bottom and is still soft on the top. Stir gently with a wooden spatula until it is cooked to your liking. Flip and fold onto a warm serving plate.

Potatoes for boys who won't eat roast!

potatoes
knob of butter

- Boil, drain, and mash with a little butter or whatever in the usual way.
- With an ice cream scoop, place scoops of potato in an oven proof dish.
- Cook gas 6, 200°C/400°F for 10-15 minutes.

Puddings

Pears with ginger

2 ripe eating pears
juice of ½ lemon
a few pieces of stem ginger
    (plus some of their syrup)
tabsp whisky

- Peel, core and slice pears.
- Brush the pears with the lemon.
- Chop the stem ginger, mix with the whisky and syrup and pour over.

"Best chilled, but if there is no time, go right ahead and eat."

Serves 2

72

bananas
chocolate buttons

Chocolate bananas

- Peel a banana and slit it along the middle, but do not cut it all the way through.
- Take some chocolate buttons and put into the banana, along the slit.
- Wrap the banana well in foil and place over the camp fire on a rack until cooked through.

For the adult version ...

bananas
favourite chocolate
rum or brandy

Barbecued bananas

- Peel and cut a slit in each banana, but not right through.
- Wedge small pieces of chocolate into the banana flesh.
- Add a dash of rum or brandy, and wrap each banana in foil.
- Heat on the barbecue for a few minutes.

Banana stand-by

2 bananas
1 dessert apple, chopped
30g raisins
15g flaked almonds
3 pieces stem ginger in
    syrup, or preserved
    ginger
2 maraschino cherries
a little ginger syrup or
    maraschino cherry juice

- Slice up bananas in a bowl and add apple, raisins, flaked almonds, chopped ginger, and maraschino cherries.
- Add a little ginger syrup or maraschino cherry juice to moisten – there must be a little liquid.
- Mush it around.
- Divide into 2 bowls and top with a cherry.

If made while the main course is cooking, by the time it is served it will have blended nicely. Goes well over ice-cream.

Clementine compote

clementines
small tin crushed pineapple
marmalade
rum

- Segment as many clementines as needed.
- In a small pan simmer a few tabsps marmalade and some crushed pineapple with a dollop of rum. Quantities depend on your fancy.
- Pour over clementines and leave to cool.

Hot orange and raisin sauce

tin mandarin oranges
   (drained)
50g raisins
15g butter
2 tabsps soft brown sugar
1 tabsp golden syrup
block of vanilla ice-cream

- Place in a saucepan all ingredients (except ice-cream!), plus a little of the tinned juice, and heat well.
- Place ice-cream straight from freezer on a serving plate, and pour the hot sauce over it. Serve speedily.

Serves 4

Swedish apricot pudding (Southlands College pudding)

250g Fair Trade dried
   apricots
50g (approx.) margarine
125g Fair Trade muscovado
   sugar
⅓ pt (approx.) whipped
   cream
cornflakes for topping

- Soak and cook apricots until soft enough to mash with a fork, and place in a glass serving bowl.
- Cover the apricots with the whipped cream.
- Melt the margarine and sugar over a low heat, then add enough cornflakes to bind.
- Cover cream with cornflake topping.

Serves 6-8

Caribbean cream

fresh fruit in bite-size pieces
    (eg pineapple, grapes)
double cream
Greek yoghurt
Demerara sugar

- Place fruit in a serving bowl.
- Mix equal quantities of double cream and Greek yoghurt (depending upon the number of people), spread on top of fruit.
- Cover with a generous layer of Demerara sugar, then cover the dish with cling film for a few hours.

Summer fruit brulée

1 tub (8oz) (200g) any
    summer fruit
½ pt (300ml) double cream
½ pt (300ml) Greek yoghurt
few drops of vanilla essence
1oz (25g) Demerara sugar

- Put fruit into a heat-proof bowl.
- Whip cream until it holds its shape.
- Add yoghurt and vanilla and mix together.
- Put over the fruit and scatter the Demerara sugar on top.
- Grill under a high heat for 3-4 minutes until sugar is caramelised – alternatively caramelise it with a cook's blow torch.

Serves 4

1 small packet sponge
    fingers
1 small bowl of very strong
    coffee, cold
tot of brandy
8oz (200g) soft cream
    cheese
½ can of ready made custard
3oz (75g) grated chocolate
whipped cream and toasted
    almonds to decorate

½pt (300ml) double cream
1 lemon
3oz (75g) caster sugar

Serves 4

Tiramisu

- Dip biscuits into coffee and line the base of a dish. Sprinkle with the brandy.
- Beat together the custard and cream cheese.
- Sprinkle half the chocolate over the sponge fingers, then cover with the cheese mixture.
- Place in fridge and chill for 6 hours or overnight.
- Finish off by sprinkling remaining chocolate over the top and decorate with whipped cream and toasted almonds.

Serves 4

Lemon cup

- Remove lemon peel as thinly as possible (without the pith), place in the cream, add the sugar and bring to the boil, stirring.
- Remove the juice from the lemon. In a bowl, strain the cream mixture over the juice and stir.
- Pour into small individual dishes and leave to set (***not*** in the fridge).
- When set, the dishes may then be placed in the fridge.

1 lemon meringue pie mix
1 lemon
2 eggs
4oz (100g) caster sugar

"Serve with shortbread fingers or langues de chat and accept the compliments!"

3 fat juicy lemons
190g icing sugar
450ml double cream
3 tabsps limoncello liqueur
   (chilled in the freezer)

Lemon fluff

- Make up the lemon part of the pie mix with 2 egg yolks, and 2 extra squeezes of lemon juice, and allow to cool.
- When cool, whisk the two egg whites with sugar into a meringue mixture.
- Fold the lemon mixture into the meringue until evenly coloured, and divide into 4-6 small bowls.
- Top with a little whipped cream and toasted almonds.

Serves 4-6

Frozen lemon dessert

- Finely grate the zest of the lemons into a bowl then add their juice.
- Stir in the sugar and leave for 30 minutes.
- Whip the cream with the ice-cold limoncello (alternatively use 3 tabsps ice-cold water - as if!!) until you have soft peaks, then beat in the lemon juice mixture.
- Turn into a I.5 litre container and pop into the freezer with no need to stir.
- Freeze for up to 7-8 hours or, ideally, overnight.

Hazelnut meringue cake

4 egg whites
9oz (225g) caster sugar
vanilla essence
½ teasp vinegar
4½oz (112g) browned ground
    hazel nuts
¼pt (150ml) cream
icing sugar and raspberries
    to finish

Serves 6-8

- Prepare two 8" sandwich tins by rubbing the sides with butter and dusting with flour, then line with Bakewell paper.
- Prepare the hazel nuts by roasting in the microwave until brown.
- Grind in a mixer (but **not** to a fine powder!).
- Whisk the egg whites until stiff and stir in the vinegar and the vanilla essence.
- Add half the sugar, whisking gently, and then fold in the rest of the sugar. Fold in the nuts.
- Fill the tins and bake for 30-40 minutes at gas 5, 190°C/375°F.
- Whip the cream and add with the raspberries between the meringues.

"The most popular pudding I have ever made – everyone likes it."

Base:

280g (10oz) ginger-nut
    biscuits
140g (5oz) butter, melted

Cheese mixture:

230g (8oz) cream cheese
150ml (¼ pint) double cream
110g (4oz) caster sugar
2 pieces stem ginger,
    chopped
1 tabsp brandy, or ginger
    syrup
2 eggs, size 3, separated
juice of 1 large lemon
1 sachet (1 level tabsp)
    gelatine
1kg (approx 2lb) loaf tin,
    lightly oiled
Plus: 6 brandy snaps
150ml (¼ pint) double cream,
    whipped

Brandy snap cheesecake

- Crush the biscuits, and stir into melted butter.
- Mix cream cheese, cream, sugar, ginger and brandy or syrup, then beat in egg yolks.
- Put lemon juice in a small pan, sprinkle gelatine over the top, leave to soak for a few minutes, then dissolve over a gentle heat (do not boil); stir into the mixture.
- Whisk egg whites, fairly stiffly, take one spoonful and stir thoroughly into the cheese mixture, then carefully fold in the rest.
- Pour half this mixture into the loaf tin and sprinkle evenly with half the biscuit mixture; add another layer each of cheese and biscuit mixtures.
- Chill the cake for several hours or overnight till set.
- To turn out, dip the tin in boiling water for a few seconds, cover with a plate and turn the whole thing over. Give a sharp shake if necessary to loosen it. Fill brandy snaps with cream and arrange them on top.

Advance preparation The cheesecake can be turned out a few hours in advance; leave the tin over it and keep in the fridge. Fill the brandy snaps for the top at the last minute, to keep them crisp. *Serves 6*

Raspberry and apple cake

225g (8oz) self raising flour
large pinch salt
175g (6oz) butter or
 margarine
50g (2oz) ground almonds
125g (4oz) caster sugar
225g (8oz) eating apples,
 peeled, cored and
 chopped
2 eggs, beaten
45ml (3 tabsps) milk
225g (8oz) raspberries or
 frozen raspberries
50g (2oz) flaked almonds

- Grease and base line a 20cm/8" spring-released cake tin.
- Sift the flour and salt into a large bowl, and rub in the butter until the mixture resembles breadcrumbs.
- Stir in the ground almonds, sugar and apples, using a wooden spoon.
- Beat in the eggs and milk, then carefully fold in half of the raspberries.
- Spoon the mixture carefully into the tin and smooth the surface. Sprinkle over the remaining raspberries and the flaked almonds.
- Bake at gas mark 4, 180°C/350°F, for about 1-1¼ hours, or until well risen, golden brown and firm to the touch in the centre.
- Dust with icing sugar and serve warm or cold on its own or with yoghurt cream or crème fraiche.

Serves 8

Quick crumble: *version 1 – soft fruit*

Use any soft fruit stored in your freezer.
cornflour
soft sugar
crumble topping
Demerara sugar

Crumble topping:
100g self raising flour
50g butter
50g caster sugar
[This quantity serves 4.]

- Butter a small ovenproof dish big enough for the number of portions you need to serve.
- In a poly bag place as much soft fruit as you think will fill the chosen dish. Add soft sugar (caster, white or golden) to taste, and a dessert-spoonful of fine cornflour. Shake together and place in dish.
- Have ready as much crumble topping as you think will be needed to top the dish. To make topping, rub butter into flour until it resembles fine breadcrumbs; stir in sugar.
- Spread crumble mixture over fruit.
- Sprinkle the top with a fine dusting of Demerara sugar.
- Bake in a hot oven, gas mark 6, 200ºC/400ºF, for about 20 minutes or until just golden and the juice is beginning to bubble up the sides.

"Serve with ice cream, cream or custard or any combination. If there is any left, it is yummy cold."

Quick crumble: *version 2 – apple*

apples, peeled and roughly
   sliced
sugar
crumble topping
2 tablespoons of porridge
   oats
ground cinnamon
lemon

[For crumble ingredients see
previous recipe.]

- Butter a small ovenproof dish big enough for the number of portions you need to serve.
- Fill dish will apple pieces. Sprinkle with sugar to taste.
- In a small poly bag, place as much crumble topping as you think will be needed to top the dish plus 2 tablespoons of porridge oats, and ground cinnamon to taste (for extra flavour add the grated rind of a lemon), shake to mix. Sprinkle this mixture over the apples.
- Bake in a medium hot oven, gas mark 4, 180°C/350°F, for about 30 minutes or until just golden and the juice is beginning to bubble up the sides.
- Serve with custard. *"A glass of sweet cider goes well with it."*

450ml carton of double
    cream
pack of broken meringues
2 Crunchie bars
2 chocolate flake bars

Crunchie ice cream

- Whip the cream.
- Add the broken meringues, the 2 Crunchie bars roughly smashed up, and the two chocolate flake bars roughly broken up.
- Fold all together, place in large plastic box and freeze.
- Serve straight from the freezer.

Simple strawberry ice cream

2 punnets strawberries
juice of one lemon
150g sugar
225ml water
150ml double cream,
    whipped

- Purée strawberries in blender.
- Add lemon juice.
- Put sugar and water into pan.
- Make syrup and cool.
- Mix syrup into strawberry pulp.
- Fold in the cream until the mixture is well blended.
- Pour into plastic containers.
- Freeze overnight.

Cakes

Microwave fruit cake

350g (12oz) mixed dry fruit
50g (2oz) chopped glace
  cherries
175g (6oz) dark brown sugar
100g (4oz) margarine
1½ x 5ml teasp mixed spice
150ml (¼pt) water
225g (8oz) self raising flour
pinch of bicarbonate of soda
1 egg, medium

- Place fruit, sugar, margarine, spice and water in a large bowl; heat for 3 minutes on **high**.
- Add flour, bicarbonate of soda and egg, and mix well. Spoon into a lined 20cm (8") round container.
- Cook for 10 minutes on **medium high** and 1 minute on **high**.
- Leave to stand in dish for 5 minutes before turning out to cool.

1 mug water
4oz (100g) margarine
2 mug self raising flour
1lb (400g) mixed fruit
1 mug sugar
2 eggs

6oz (175g) self raising flour
6oz (175) Demerara sugar
8oz (225g) mixed dried fruit
2 eggs, beaten
4oz (110g) margarine
½ teasp vanilla essence
½ teasp almond essence

*"Very easy, and lovely
buttered or with cheese."*

Boiled fruit cake 1

- Pre-heat the oven to gas 2, 150ºC/300ºF.
- Put margarine, fruit, sugar, and water in a large pan. Bring to the boil and simmer for 15 minutes.
- Leave to cool by placing the pan in a bowl of cold water.
- Add the eggs and the flour to the pan, and beat well.
- Pour into a 7"-8" greased cake tin, place in oven and bake for 2 hours.

Boiled fruit cake 2

- Cover fruit with water and boil for 5 minutes.
- Strain well, place in a bowl, then add margarine to fruit and chop in with a knife.
- Add beaten eggs, sugar and essences.
- Sift in flour and mix well together.
- Put mixture into a greased 2lb/1kg loaf tin and bake gas mark 3, 170ºC/325ºF for approx. 1 hour.
- Turn out and leave to cool on a wire rack.

Harvest fruit loaf

4oz (100g) margarine
4oz (100g) caster sugar
8oz (200g) self raising
    flour
2 eggs
¼pt (150ml) milk
12oz (300g) mixed fruit
1 teasp mixed spice

- Put all ingredients into a bowl and beat until well mixed.
- Grease and line the base of a 2lb loaf tin, and put in the loaf mixture.
- Bake in oven on middle shelf at gas mark 4, 180°C/350°

Cooking time approx. 1½ hours

Margam's currant cake

8oz (200g) butter
8oz (200g) granulated sugar
2 eggs
10oz (250g) self raising flour
rind of 1 lemon
a little milk
8oz (200g) currants

- Put butter and sugar into mixer and beat until well mixed and soft.
- Add eggs, one at a time, also add the lemon rind.
- Add flour and, if necessary, moisten with a little milk.
- Lastly add currants.
- Turn the mixture into a greased cake tin.
- Bake at gas mark 4, 180°C/350°F for 1-1½ hours until the centre is firm.

87

8oz (200g) self-raising flour, plus spices – dried mixed spice, ginger, cinnamon, nutmeg (about 2 teasp in total)
8oz (200g) margarine
8oz (200g) soft dark brown sugar
4 eggs at room temperature
2½lb (1kg) mixed dried fruit in total (can include peel, chopped glacé cherries, ginger, dried apricots, dates, and chopped nuts)
2 tabsps milk
3 tabsps brandy

In advance:
For best results, spread over two days, by soaking dried fruits in brandy overnight.

Christmas cake

- This amount makes two 7" round cakes or one 8" square cake.
- Prepare cake tin(s) and set oven to gas 3; 160°C/325°F.
- Weigh and soften the margarine (*"beat it into submission"*).
- Add sugar and beat vigorously until soft and airy.
- Add 1 egg and beat it lightly into mixture.
- Add a little flour / spices, then bit by bit the other eggs, and the rest of the flour. If the mixture seems a bit dry, add a little milk.
- Fold in the soaked fruit, and turn mixture into tin(s).
- To cook round cakes: middle shelf, side by side: gas mark 3, 160°C/325°F, for 1 hour, then gas 2, 150°C/300°F, for 1¾ hours.
- To cook square cake: gas mark 3, 160°C/325°F for 1½ hours, then gas mark 2, 150°C/300°F, for 2 hours.

Leave to cool before turning out.

Quick rich chocolate cake

Very rich, as much a pudding as a cake; it should still be slightly soft in the centre when removed from the oven.

250g dark chocolate (around 70% cocoa solids), broken into chunks
250g unsalted butter, cut into cubes
4 medium eggs, separated
100g caster mixed with l00g light muscovado sugar
50g plain flour
50g ground almonds

- Preheat the oven to gas mark 3, 170°C/325°F, and line a 23cm Springform cake tin with baking parchment.
- Put the chocolate and butter in a bowl and melt over a pan of just simmering water.
- Meanwhile, whisk the egg yolks with the sugar until well combined.
- Stir the melted chocolate and butter into the egg and sugar mixture.
- Combine the flour and almonds, then stir into the mixture.
- Whisk the egg whites until they hold firm peaks. Stir a spoonful of egg white into the chocolate mixture to loosen it, then fold in the rest with a large metal spoon, keeping in as much air as possible.
- Pour into the tin and bake for 30 minutes, or until only just set in the centre.

Serve warm or cold.

6oz (150g) margarine
6oz (150g) caster sugar
6oz (150g) self raising
  flour
3 eggs
2 tablespoons milk
rind of one lemon

For the drizzle:
2oz (50g) caster sugar
juice of one lemon

½lb (200g) SR flour
3oz (75g) sugar
2oz (50g) sultanas
½lb (200g) chopped
  apples
3oz (75g) butter
a little milk

Lemon drizzle cake

- Pre-heat oven to gas mark 4, 180°C/350°F.
- Line a 2lb loaf tin with greased greaseproof paper.
- Cream margarine and sugar. Beat eggs. Mix eggs into creamed mixture, a little at a time. Sieve flour and beat into mixture. Add lemon rind and milk.
- Put into tin. Cook for about 60 minutes and check.
- Leave cake to get fairly cool.
- Mix sugar with the lemon juice; stir in well to make sure all sugar is dissolved. Slit cake in several places and drizzle in the juice slowly. Leave cake to get completely cold.

Dorset apple cake

- Rub fat into flour and mix in all other ingredients, plus a pinch of salt, making into firm dough with the milk.
- Bake in a greased 7"-8" tin in a moderate oven, gas mark 4, 180°C/350°F, for c.45 minutes, and check.
- Serve hot, split and buttered, or with cream.

4oz (100g) soft margarine or
   unsalted butter
6oz (150g) golden caster
   sugar
6oz (150g) self-raising flour
1 teasp baking powder
2 very large eggs
4 tabsps milk
grated rind of 1 unwaxed
   lemon
2oz (50g) grated chocolate
   (white or brown)

For the topping:
4oz (100g) chocolate –
   white or whatever
2oz (50g) unsalted butter
Fruit jellies *or* Dolly
   Mixtures *or* Smarties

Amélie's jewel cake

- Put all the ingredients for the cake into a bowl and beat till smooth.
- Pour into a greased and paper-lined 7" round cake tin.
- Bake at gas mark 4, 180°C/350°F for 40 minutes *or* until an inserted skewer comes out clean.
- Cool totally **in tin**.

Icing:
- Melt the chocolate in a bowl over warm water, add butter and stir till all is melted and combined.
- Pour icing onto cake, smooth over the surface, decorate with chosen sweeties and then enjoy.

"Absolutely scrummy"

Camp fire dough nuts

bread and jam for sandwiches
pancake batter mix
oil for frying
a little sugar

- Make the jam sandwiches and cut them into quarters.
- Make up the pancake batter mix and pour into a deep plate.
- Coat the sandwiches in the batter, both sides.
- Fry in hot oil in the frying pan (over the fire if you are out of doors) turning until brown.
- Sprinkle with sugar and serve.

Katherine's cupcakes

2 eggs
4oz (100g) self-raising
     flour
4oz (100g) soft butter
4oz (100g) caster sugar

- Sift the flour into a large bowl, then add the eggs, butter and sugar.
- Stir everything together until it is smooth.
- Put paper cases on a baking tray, then, using two teaspoons, spoon the mixture into the paper cases.
- Bake in the oven at gas 4, 180ºC (350ºF), for about 15-20 minutes until the cakes are golden brown.
- Allow to cool … *"and then they are ready to be iced, decorated, and eaten!"*

Rosie's carrot and orange muffins

4 medium eggs
6 tabsp caster sugar
5oz (175g) self raising
    wholemeal flour
2 teasps mixed spice
8oz (200g) grated carrot
grated rind of an orange

- Whisk the eggs and the sugar together until pale and creamy.
- Sift the flour and mixed spice together and gently fold in.
  Fold in carrot and orange.
- Spoon into muffin cases and bake at gas mark 5, 190ºC/375ºF.
- Cook for 20 – 25 minutes, until well risen.

Biscuits

8oz (200g) margarine
6oz (150g) sugar
10oz (250g) self raising flour
1 egg
vanilla
pinch of salt
2oz (50g) cornflakes

Cornflake biscuits

- Mix everything except cornflakes together by hand or by mixer.
- Roll into small balls, then coat with lightly crushed cornflakes.
- Place on baking sheet and bake until golden at gas mark 5, 190ºC/375ºF.

"Very useful for coffee mornings, fêtes, bazaars etc."

Yummy choc biscuits

4oz (100g) butter/margarine
2oz (50g) caster sugar
4oz (100g) self raising flour
1oz (25g) cocoa powder
few drops vanilla essence

For the butter cream:
2oz (50g) butter/margarine
4oz (100g) icing sugar
2 tabsps hot water
1 tabsp cocoa

- Heat oven, gas 5, 190°C/375°F.
- Cream together butter and sugar until light and fluffy.
- Stir in flour, coca and vanilla essence.
- Roll 24 balls of the mixture of equal size in the hand, the size of a marble. Flatten a bit with a fork on to the tray.
- Bake 10 minutes and cool on a wire rack.
- Cream together the butter cream ingredients.
- When biscuits are cold, sandwich in pairs with the butter cream filling and dust with icing sugar.

Makes 12 biscuits

Grantham ginger biscuits

4oz (100g) self-raising flour
1 teasp ginger
2oz (50g) margarine
1 teasp bicarbonate of soda
2oz (50g) sugar
1 tabsp syrup

- Melt syrup and margarine in a saucepan, and add to dry ingredients in a bowl. Mix well.
- Make into small flattened balls and bake in a moderate oven gas mark 4, 350°F/180°C for 15 minutes.

Rebeccas currant biscuits

8oz (225g) of plain flour
4oz (110g) of caster sugar
4oz (110g) of butter or
    margarine
2oz (50g) currants
1 medium egg beaten
1 teasp water
a little caster sugar to
    sprinkle

- Pre-heat oven to gas mark 4, 350ºF/180ºC.
- Mix flour, sugar and butter in a bowl.
- Add the currants, beaten egg and water.
- Roll out to about 6mm (¼") thick.
- Using a fluted 60mm (2½") cutter, stamp out the biscuits.
- Place on an oiled baking sheet and sprinkle with caster sugar.
- Bake for about 15 minutes.
- Cool on a wire rack.

8oz or 225g of Plain flour
4oz or 110g of butter or margarine
4oz or 110g of caster sugar
2oz of currants (50g)
1 medium egg beaten
1 tea Spoon of water
a little caster sugar to sprinkle
Pre-heat the oven to gas mark 4 (350°f) (180°c)

96

Extras

12 large tomatoes, peeled
1lb (400g) brown sugar
4 large onions
1 tabsp dry mustard
handful salt
1 tabsp curry powder
5 chillies (according to taste)
2 heaped tabsps flour
vinegar, at least a pint
    (600ml).

NB: needs 2 days

Tomato relish

- Cut tomatoes into chunks, sprinkle with the salt and leave over night.
- Next day pour off the accumulated liquid and put tomatoes and onions, roughly chopped, into a pan with sugar and chillies (in a muslin bag). Add enough vinegar to cover.
- Bring to the boil and simmer 1½ hours.
- Mix flour, curry powder and mustard to a paste with cold vinegar. Add to mixture and boil five minutes.
- Put into jars and cover when cold.

Pesto

2oz (50g) fresh basil leaves
1 large clove garlic, sliced
1 tabsp pine kernels
6 tabsps extra virgin olive oil
salt
1oz (25g) parmesan cheese

- Put basil, garlic, pine kernels and salt in a processor and whiz.
- Slowly pour in the oil.
- Finally stir in the grated cheese, if using immediately.

The sauce will keep for a day or two in the fridge and freeze well without the parmesan.
Can be used to give a real zing to salads, pasta and fish.

Salad cream

1 tabsp sugar
1 good teasp cornflour
scant teasp salt
2 tabsps (30ml) oil
1 egg, beaten
1 good teasp made mustard
6 tabsps (90ml) milk
4 tabsps (60ml) vinegar

- Mix dry ingredients; add oil, beaten egg and mustard.
- Lastly add milk and vinegar alternately.
- Cook in double saucepan, stirring frequently until thick.

Simple green tomato chutney

1½lb (600g) green tomatoes
(can be red if using them
up)
1½lb (600g) apples
1½lb (600g) onions
1½lb (600g) white sugar
(granulated)
1pt (600ml) spiced vinegar
6oz (150g) sultanas
1 teasp-(ish) ginger or mixed
spice

- Chop and simmer in a preserving pan the tomatoes, onions and apples, for ½ hour.
- Add sugar and sultanas and cook for further ½ hour.
- Pour into warmed glass jars.

Bob's quince jelly

6lbs (2.4k) quinces,
peeled and cored
6 pts water (3.6l)
sugar
juice of ½ lemon

- Boil the chopped quinces until the quinces are well softened.
- Sieve through a jelly bag or muslin.
- Measure the liquor and add ¾lb sugar to 1pt liquor, then add lemon juice.
- Boil until the liquor reaches setting point.
- Pot in small jars. *Makes about 12 jars*

Blackcurrant jam

"If you like the idea of homemade jam but are not into sugar thermometers and standing over a hot stove, then this is for you."

1lb (400g) washed
    blackcurrants
(or any other berries you
    have growing around the
    garden)
1lb (400g) sugar
1 tabsp lemon juice
4 tabsp of water

- Place fruit in a large bowl, cover and microwave for three minutes.
- Stir well then add sugar and microwave for five minutes.
- Stir and cook for a further 13 minutes. *"I normally do five and five and three stirring in between."*
- Leave to cool, and then pour into pots.

Comments: This recipe is based on a 650w oven. The same technique can be used with whatever you have growing in the garden: redcurrants, strawberries, raspberries, gooseberries, blackberries.

"Blackcurrant just happens to be the favourite in our house. As for how long it keeps... depends on who's around!"

Making Life Easier

Electricity cuts effort! Our cooks were asked to name their favourite piece of electrical equipment.

The most popular item: hand held electric whisk
A close second: a liquidizer/blender, either hand held or free standing

Most frequently mentioned large items:

Food mixer (Kenwood most often named)   Food processor (Magimix)

Other recommendations included:

Breadmaker *"it's lovely to have a fresh loaf and the kitchen smells wonderful"*
Slow cooker
George Foreman grill

Juicer/lemon squeezer
The kitchen radio!
The kettle

"I wouldn't be without .... "

Professional cooks stress the necessity of sharp knives, and often lay out what can seem a daunting (and expensive) range. However, it is worth noting that, among our contributors, the most frequent reference by far is to a favourite **'small sharp knife',** for chopping, peeling vegetables etc. (eg *"the one your brother-in-law gave me as a Xmas present years ago"*).

Otherwise, only a few items were mentioned more than once:

wooden spoon

spatula

favourite potato peeler
(eg IKEA)

knife sharpener
(*"given me by my butcher years ago"*)

balloon (or other hand-held) whisk

bowls, in various sizes and plenty of them

Other items mentioned:

apple corer

bean shredder

cheese slicer (*"stops me eating too much"*)

chopping boards

cling film

colander

compost small bin or bucket (lidded)

digital scales

fingers!

foil

grater

garlic press (*"a good one"*)

heavy gauge plastic bags
(*"for pouring and storing – self-standing and re-sealable, for stews, soups, and casseroles"*)

herb chopper

kitchen scissors

lemon/orange zester

meat thermometer

mouli-legume

oven dishes

pasta draining spoon

pastry brush with rubber bristles
(*"which don't fall out!"*)

plastic measuring spoons
(*"out of a Xmas cracker ten years ago!"*)

shaped cutters

timer (*"invaluable for multi-tasking – try to get one you can wear round your neck!"*)

tongs

vegetable peeler (swivel-headed)

wall-fixed knife sharpener.

Most of these items are not expensive and can be collected over time relatively painlessly.

Our contributors commend... Our cooks were asked to nominate the cookery writer whom they had found the most helpful.

The overwhelming favourite was **Delia Smith,** through the successive phases of her publishing career. No one else came anywhere near her.

Other writers with **more than one nomination** were:

Mrs Beeton (in her various published guises)	Ainsley Harriott	Constance Spry & Rosemary Hume
Mary Berry	Nigella Lawson	Katie Stewart
Elizabeth David	Jamie Oliver	
	Gordon Ramsay	

Other nominations include:

Robert Carrier	Pat Hesketh (WI adviser)	James Martin
Louise Davies	Linda McCartney	Claudia Roden
Jane Grigson	Claire Macdonald	Nigel Slater

Treasured cook books: Hardly any two contributors nominated the same book, but there were some trends:

- A good 'comprehensive' cookery book, acquired early in one's cooking career, remains a friend for life.
- illustrated books featured strongly.
- compilations by organisations (eg WI, food institutes, magazines, manufacturers' recipe books) find favour with many.
- thematic books (eg, vegetarian, dairy, preserves) are popular.
- *"Books which are good to read, as much as to cook from."*

Almost effortless? Planning and shopping. Nigella Lawson makes the case that planning and shopping are the most stressful parts of providing the meals.

A staggering range of ingredients is now available in supermarkets and elsewhere, some of them very exotic, and a vast number of recipes for deploying them are to be found in celebrity and specialist recipe books. The risk is that some expensive item will be little used, and what is left over will be wasted.

For the most part, the recipes in this book collectively draw upon a range of ingredients used fairly frequently. A weekly supermarket swoop would find nearly everything.

Developing a real interest in cooking tends to lead to an increased interest in the source of the ingredients. This soon topples over into the vast debate about the production of food globally, air-miles and carbon foot-prints, the power of the supermarkets, organic produce, intensive farming, animal welfare, and Fair Trade.

All this can be rather daunting when you are simply trying to feed the family, and is beyond the scope of this book; however, it is fair to suggest that the more the taste of food becomes a priority, the greater the likelihood that it will generate increased interest in reliable sourcing, especially of fish, meat and dairy products, and in locally grown fruit and vegetables. This is not 'earth mother' stuff but a modest attempt to increase our control of our food.

The great thing about being the cook is that you know what you and the family are actually eating – no need to peer at the minuscule print on the packets of made up meals for e-numbers, salt, sugar, fats and the like – or to wonder whether the meat can only be called 'British' because the final meal was prepared in the UK.

Among the suggestions put forward by our contributors are:

- building up your knowledge of good local suppliers, box deliveries and so on, as well as of favourite specialist companies by post.

- making a menu plan for the week ahead or whatever, before going shopping. (You may well vary it as the week proceeds, but it reduces waste as well as those 'What on earth am I going to feed them tonight?' moments.)

- keeping a place in the kitchen (eg a clip-board or under a fridge magnet) for noting the items you are running out of. This list and the menu list can then form the basis of the shopping trip.

- checking the relevant recipes before you go shopping to ensure that you get everything necessary (this from a man).

- if time and opportunity permit, checking the internet sites of the major supermarkets for bargains and price information.

- bulk buying, especially for the freezer, which represents a notable saving.

- buying ingredients as and when you need them, not because you have been seduced by cookery writers into assuming that a real cook must have such and such an item in the larder.

Planning and shopping offer the real trade-off between expenditure of time and effort on the one hand, and cost on the other. Two of our contributors share their experience on pages 113 and 115.

Almost effortless? **The store cupboard and so on.** The helpful lists compiled by cookery editors can sometimes seem rather daunting. But some stores there must be; as Katherine Whitehorn put it in her book *Cooking in a Bedsitter*, a boiled egg would be ruinously expensive if you had to buy a packet of salt every time you had one!

One of the benefits of a well maintained store cupboard, fridge and freezer is that shopping for specific ingredients for a recipe may mean buying only one or two items *because all the other ingredients are likely to be to hand already.*

While one cook's necessities will be another's extravagances, a reasonable range in store also means that there can always be something on the table even at short notice, or for unexpected visitors.

It is only too easy to lose sight of what you already have. (Countless mothers have looked into the fridge in their offspring's shared student accommodation, and wondered where they went wrong in bringing them up!) It makes economic sense to keep an eye on what's to hand; food still in good condition is usable, thereafter it is wasted.

Only you can judge how methodical to be. You can have a system for rotating purchases or you can reckon that at some point you will be down to your last tin of sardines before buying in a fresh supply, in which case storing in date order is superfluous.

The advice that when you have a quiet time you should make meals to freeze is sound – if you ever have the spare time. If not, try doubling up the recipe for an immediate meal, eg for a casserole, and freezing half of it or whatever, for future use. For a comprehensive approach to keep in store, see page 109.

Almost effortless? Clearing up. No easy answers – but our cooks offered a number of suggestions:

- Classifying kitchen rubbish (eg tins, bottles, etc) is now an obligation on all of us. A proper system which works for you limits time and frustration.

- If you collect vegetable matter for composting, a special container is a help, placed to hand on the work surface (anything from an old colander to a purpose-made crock pot with charcoal filter).

- A bowl of hot soapy water in the sink during cooking makes for easy rinsing of utensils; filling a dirty pan with water and soaking it overnight makes for almost effortless cleaning in the morning.

- Beware just piling dirty crocks and pans into the sink and leaving them – as Shirley Conran remarks, this is a practice sometimes adopted by helpful guests (OK, she says men!), who appear never to have reached into the cold greasy water later to extract them.

- Getting everything into the dishwasher fast immediately makes the kitchen look better and any remaining items less daunting.

- Some of the recipes use a single oven dish or saucepan; as one contributor put it *"One bowl recipes are a boon with a baby"*. In other recipes the cooking time allows for any clearing up to be out of the way before eating.

- In addition to non-stick utensils, enamel is a great medium for easy cleaning.

- Mail order suppliers and supermarkets offer a huge range of cleaning materials, often not cheap. Salt, vinegar, lemon juice and bicarbonate of soda, all work excellently well, in various contexts.

- If the men offer to take their turn, (eg during the Christmas festivities) accept enthusiastically. Just don't stand around in the kitchen, telling them how to do it!

- How much you clear up as you go along is up to you; if you have the space to absorb the clutter and prefer to concentrate on the cooking itself, especially when dealing with an elaborate meal, there is no moral law which says that you must keep the kitchen tidy as you proceed.

Finally, two opposing views:

a) *NEVER go to bed leaving the clearing up to be done.*

b) *ALTERNATIVELY, don't spoil the atmosphere of a good meal shared with friends or whoever, by fretting about the dirty dishes. Just put leftovers into appropriate store swiftly and discreetly, and tackle the rest in due course, next day if you are too tired at night.*

FOOD FOR THOUGHT: THREE COOKS SHARE THEIR APPROACH

1. Stores & Equipment

The Store-cupboard/Larder

The good old 'stand-bys' are ever necessary in whatever cooking environment – from huge kitchen to caravan – the basic things to help out at times of "emergency" are reasonably easy to source.

- ***Tins*** Chopped and whole tomatoes, with and without the additions of garlic and herbs; baked beans, sweet-corn, different types of beans (flageolet, canellini, borlotti, red kidney and chick peas); tinned fruits (*in natural juice*), evaporated milk. Fish – tuna and sardines are the most versatile. Meat – stewed steak and ham.
- ***Packets*** Custard, different pastas, sugars (once the big packet is half empty, decant into smaller jars *or* plastic seal boxes that stack more easily). Porridge oats are not just for breakfast. Various types of rice – easy cook, basmati and risotto. Sugar free jelly.
- ***Jars*** Jars of different patés are very useful. Good jams and spreads make good toppings for puddings *or* special sauces for meats.
- ***Bottles*** Soy sauce, chilli sauce, stock powders (reduced salt where possible), flavoured vinegars. (Try walnut vinegar with walnut oil for a simple dressing.)

- *Herbs and Spices* – the golden rule is **DATE the jar when you open it and take note of the keeping life guidelines on the jar** … we've all got jars of "odd" herbs and spices that we bought for that special recipe years ago – throw them out; they will be worse than none at all. Keep things like black peppercorns/dried mixed herbs and "herbes de provence" (not the same thing), dried sage and thyme (if you are really lucky – freeze your own in the glut season) and a selection of the sweet spices: cinnamon, ground ginger, paprika and turmeric.
- *Salt*   A controversial issue! I keep both table and cooking salt, *and* coarse sea salt.

The Freezer

The biggest help of all can be your freezer – if you are a fan of freezing leftovers, can you think of making them into something super *before* you freeze? All too often, leftovers actually get forgotten and in the long term are thrown away.

- Keep a bag of basic crumble mix (not sweetened – you can always add grated cheese and dried mixed herbs for a quick savoury topping to fish *or* meat mixtures).
- Keep a bag of basic scone topping without the liquid element – again great for quick topping for pies – sweet or savoury.
- Frozen vegetables – peas are invaluable for all sorts of dishes. Frozen beans of all types, and sweet-corn. Keep bags of sliced, diced and chopped onion – red and white, invaluable for a quick meal.
- A bag of breadcrumbs – make them by placing stale bread in your food-processor (I don't use crusts as it makes the crumbs a strange colour when you are making bread sauce!).

If you like to use crusts, keep in a separate bag and make into crumbs as needed *or* use for smashing down for a coarse topping.

- A bag of small frozen fish fillets – white fish and/or salmon.
- Always convert your chicken carcase into stock – see recipe on page 16
- Freeze fruit when in season and, if you live in an area where fruit trees abound, ***never*** turn down the offer of excess fruit from your neighbour.
  - *Apples*   peel, core, quarter or segment, blanch in acidulated water, bag and freeze. Purée without sweetener *or* butter, freeze in tubs *or* ice-cube container.
  - *Pears*   peel, core, quarter or segment, blanch in acidulated water, bag and freeze.
  - *Plums*   wash, de-stone and freeze.
  - *Raspberries*   lay whole fruit on trays and 'open freeze' on trays lined with baking parchment; when frozen, tip into bags or boxes and label. Any that are not whole, purée with a little lemon juice (helps to keep the colour) and a teaspoon of icing sugar – if you want to be really smart push through a fine sieve. Use this purée as a topping sauce for ice-cream or to decorate any pudding.
  - *Strawberries*   wipe, don't wash! – and then as raspberries.
  - *Blackberries*   as raspberries.

The Fridge

Tubs of mixed herbs in oil: garlic/ginger/lemongrass/chilli; and that good old standby, tomato purée (sun-dried or ordinary), lime pickle, mayonnaise (good quality – did you know you can cook it?); jars of different mustards – wholegrain, Dijon, and any others that find their way back from the continent – great for flavouring mayonnaise for a quick accompaniment to grilled meat or fish.

A Note On Equipment

Chopping Boards - I keep different colour boards for different functions. They are all plastic and easily go in the dishwasher.

Food Processor –it really does make life easy and is a great time saver.

Good knives – don't have to be wildly expensive *but* they do have to be sharp. Blunt knives slip and cut you.

Sieves – I have five: small conical, small shallow round, medium shallow round, large shallow round, and a large flat-bottomed sieve. I like to have the metal type – they go in the dishwasher easily!

Stick blender – easily transportable when you go on a self-catering holiday.

Steamer – electric or stove top.

Tub/form rings – keep the small plastic tubs that frozen / microwave puddings come in – they make great forms for presenting vegetables and rice.

2. Cooking For One

The challenge: much fresh food in supermarkets is packed for two or more people. (Of course, if you have a handy butcher or green grocer, where you can buy one chop or half a small cabbage, that's fine; but it's less common nowadays.) It can be boring to eat the same dish three days in a row, and fresh greens or salad produce can easily deteriorate before they are used up. An organic vegetable box can also be more than enough for one.

My solution: categorise fresh and frozen items according to keeping qualities. For me that means:

- fresh root vegetables, enough for several meals;
- frozen vegetables (peas, green beans, cauliflower, sliced mushrooms etc) which can be drawn upon as little or as much as is needed;
- High quality frozen mince is a great standby, eg for shepherd's pie or chilli con carne.

Cost: To get value for money, stock up on items used regularly when they are on offer. Resist the temptation of 2 for 1 unless you can freeze 1 or feel like a cooking spree, to include what will then be frozen. It may seem obvious, but a quick check on cupboard, fridge, and freezer before going shopping really does pay dividends.

My basic store cupboard:

tinned tomatoes	bacon	flour
chilli beans	dried fruit	sugar
rice and pasta	stock cubes	margarine

Spices: cinnamon, garam masala, ginger, ground coriander, mixed spice, nutmeg,

Herbs: dried bay leaves, thyme, herbes de Provence,

Fresh root ginger: peeled and cut into small chunks of the size used for most dishes, freezes very well.

Grow your own: fresh mint, thyme, rosemary and sage grow well and are worth it. A pot of parsley translated into the garden may last months.

Cooking: A cold wet miserable day is just right for a cooking spree – warms the house, banishes the blues, and smells good too. Batch cooking is also economical on fuel. On a lesser level, cook two, eat one and freeze one is a useful habit.

Freezing: I use small flat containers (eg margarine tubs), which stack well, de-frost relatively quickly, and are the right size for one. For unexpected visitors, you just use as many as are needed.

Arrangements along these lines ensure that I have something nutritious and tasty to hand when I am tired, and available for guests or those who linger on till supper time.
A little lateral thinking means that hardly anything need be wasted.

3. Good Food on a Budget

Recession? Yes; and some families are badly affected by it. Austerity? No; there is no shortage of any item we have become accustomed to having. Food is available in abundance. How you shop, where you shop remains your choice. But if the budget is tight, bear in mind that expensive is not necessarily best. Don't look down your nose at economy shops; go in and judge for yourself.

As much as one third can be saved quite easily by shopping around. Try to use all the local shops and supermarkets within practicable reach – local 'small' shops will have bargains, and their owners can be very sympathetic if it's apparent that you cook. It's your money that you are spending; what you get for it depends upon you.

Buy goods when on offer; set a price at which you buy and what quantity you expect to get for that amount (being realistic). The five recipes which follow and their cost are a few examples of what can be produced by utilising *what* is on offer, *when* it is on offer.

Cox's orange apples poached in lemon and syrup
Cox's orange apples, peeled, cored and cut into chunky slices. Put the apples in a pan, add juice of 1 lemon, and ½ cup of golden syrup. Bring quickly to boil, turn off heat, put lid on pan and leave to soften in their own heat.

Apple in a flan case with glaze

Pre-bake flan case using basic 'sweet' (prepared) short crust pastry. Arrange cooled apple (as in previous recipe) around the case. Add clear gel mix to juice and spread over the apples.

Vegetarian deep quiche

Prepare basic shortcrust pastry and line a dish, adjusting your quantities to the size of dish and the number to be served. Layer: finely sliced, blanched leeks, grated cheese, lightly fried onion, tomato slices. Repeat twice. Beat four eggs with 1 pt milk, plus salt, pepper, mustard, and then dried herbs. Add 1 teaspoon each of chives, dill (if to hand), parsley, and mix. If you have it, a dash of cream is good. Pour the mixture over the layered vegetables, place in oven and bake for 45-60 minutes on gas mark 5, 190°C / 375°F. Test that the flan is set before removing it from oven. Top with finely sliced and blanched spring onion.

Bacon and mushroom flan.

Prepare basic shortcrust pastry and line flan dish. Layer: sliced mushrooms, bacon fried with onions, blanched leeks, grated cheese. Do this twice over. Beat 4 eggs, with 1 pt milk and season with salt, pepper, mustard and 1 teaspoon dried dill. Finish with cheese and a line of mushroom halves down the centre. Place in oven for 45-60 minutes, on gas mark 5, 190°C / 375°F, and test that the flan is set before removing from oven.
Serve quiche and flan hot or cold.

Cream of mushroom soup

Peel mushrooms and chop roughly, and keep a few small pieces aside. Fry one large onion in 1 tabsp of oil plus 2 oz butter, until lightly glazed. Add mushrooms and 1 pint water. Bring to boil and simmer until tender. Add 1 pt milk, 1 tabsp flour, and 2 good quality chicken stock cubes. Liquidize everything.

Return to heat and bring to boil. Stirring with a whisk to prevent thickening on the base of the pan, simmer until flour is thoroughly cooked. Add small mushroom pieces and cook for 2-3 minutes. Serve hot, adding a final dash of cream if you wish.

Illustrative cost: principal ingredients used and their purchase prices [at Nov. 2009]:

	£		£
Cheese (2 blocks for 1 = 800g)		Onions (3 large - mild)	0.39
(Only 1 block used)	3.50	Oranges (6 large)	0.69
Leeks (pack)	0.49	Tomatoes (large - vine)	0.99
Apples (Cox's) 7-9 bag x 2	1.18	Spring onions (bunch)	0.39
Mushrooms (box)	0.59	Pack bacon pieces 1kg (used in cubes)	
Big Lion eggs (l0)	0.99		1.99
Milk (2.25 litres)	0.99		

A nd a last thought – how to skin a rabbit!

Where cooking is concerned, at least in wealthy countries, now is the age of convenience, so much so that cooking can be avoided altogether. In many parts of the world, life is still much harder. An African recipe in the *Cookbook of the Lambeth Conference* (1988) begins *"Grind enough maize for five to seven days ..."*. For those who do choose to cook in the Western world, the amount of pre-preparation undertaken by others allows us to fit in cooking alongside many necessities and interests.

Forget sentimentality about the good old days. As that doyenne of cooks, Elizabeth David, put it: would anyone making a Christmas pudding – who had shredded suet, cleaned currants, stoned raisins and pounded spices – ever wish to do so again? But if you want to extend your range, below are the instructions on the almost effortless way to skin a rabbit, as given to the editor by a farmer's wife in Aust. Thank you, Janet, for your expertise.

- *Check the source of your rabbit – it may have shot in it. On no account use a milky doe!*
- *Paunch your rabbit immediately.*
- *Loosen the skin by putting your hand between the skin and the flesh over the hind quarters and push the legs up through and under the skin.*
- *Cut the skin around the hock to release it. After releasing both legs, hang the rabbit from a nail or hook, and it will be possible to pull the entire skin off. "This is very easy once you get the hang of it."*
- *Remove head and feet, and cook according to taste. (Bearing in mind the point about shot, it is best to avoid putting currants in the stuffing!)*

Thanks and acknowledgements

This book has been made possible by the generous willingness of the contributors to respond to the request for recipes and other information, for their patience with follow-up inquiries, and for the readiness of some to be photographed.

Particular thanks are due to:

- Tessa Floyd, Cora Mason and Sue Mealing for reading and commenting on the recipes, and for their advice on the book as a whole;

- Janet Ford for *Stores & Equipment*, Diana Everest for *Cooking for One*, and Olga Riddiford for *Good food on a budget*, and for their handsome contribution to the recipes.

For their generous sponsorship, we acknowledge:

- Siân and Brian Haynes, with whom the idea of an almost effortless cook book originally emerged;

- Anonymous sponsorship received in memory of a very good friend, the late Elaine Moore.

Our thanks go to every contributor: Beverley Barton, Des Bassett, Cynthia Black, Jane Bradshaw, Diana St J Brooks, Brownies (1st Olveston), Saffia Bullock, Gill Carne, Sally Chudley, Rosemary Clews, Frances Coleman, Harriet Croft, Sue Culpan, Gill Denning, Gina Dobbins, Anne Dyke, Diana Everest, Sue Farr, Gill Ferguson, Tessa Floyd, Janet Ford, Pat Forrest, Mary Frost[†], Janet Gilpin, Margaret Gooday, John Green, Mary Griffith, Avril Hardie, Maureen Harris, Diana Harwood[†], Joan Hawkins, Brian Haynes, Siân Haynes, Kate Hickman,

Pat Hinton, Kirsty Honey, Brenda Jones, Yvonne Jones, Katherine Livingstone, Shirley McCleavy, Angela Macquiban, Ernest Marvin, Cora Mason, John Mason, Colin Mealing, Sue Mealing, Betty Morgan, Irene Parsons, Margaret Phillips, Lizzie Philpott, Rebecca Preedy, Olga Riddiford, Susie Roberts, Alison Rowe, Wendy Savage, Tanya Sheasby, Robert Slade, Sian Slade, Maggie Spooner, Rosie Spooner, Janet Spratt, Jean Spratt, Anne Stennett, Dorothy Stoppard, Chris Varney, Val Warren, Ruth Whiting, Finola Wilson, Pauline Wright.

To these must added some respondents who left no name.

Centre page photographs:
Brian Haynes, Tessa Floyd, Janet Ford,
Katherine Livingstone, Rebecca Preedy, Amélie Jenkins,
Maggie Spooner, Janet Gilpin, Yvonne Jones, Alison and Philip Rowe,
Margaret Phillips, Diana Everest, Finola Wilson, Beverley Barton,
Sian Slade, Pauline Wright, Cora Mason, John Mason, Sally Chudley, Sue Farr,
Ernest Marvin, Kirsty Honey, Betty Morgan, Colin Mealing, Sue Mealing, Janet Spratt,
Harriet Croft, Pat Forrest, Des Bassett, Joanna Sawyer,
Rosie Spooner, Jean Spratt, Susie Roberts, Tanya Sheasby, John Green.

Index

Soup as a Meal

Soups

Starters

Vegetables

Vegetarian